I0008085

MICROSOFT 365 Copilot

The Intelligent Workplace: AI Tools for Enhanced Productivity

Savannah Johnson

MICROSOFT 365 Copilot

The Intelligent Workplace: AI Tools for Enhanced Productivity

Published by
Savannah Johnson

ISBN
9798308091592

TABLE OF CONTENTS

Imagine you're an explorer, standing at the edge of a vast, uncharted territory. That's how I felt when I first glimpsed the possibilities of AI in productivity. For years, I, like many of you, navigated the complex world of office work, wrestling with emails, data, and deadlines, feeling like there was always more to do and never enough time to accomplish it. We've all experienced the frustration of repetitive tasks that seem to steal our most valuable hours, time that could be spent on more meaningful work, on creative problem-solving, or on strategic planning. The promise of technology always seems to be just a little out of reach. We often hear whispers of the next great tool, and yet, many times, the change seems minor. But now, we are on the cusp of something genuinely revolutionary.

What if I told you, the future of work is not only about using more powerful computers or faster internet connections? What if the next revolution lies in smarter software that is capable of understanding and adapting to our needs, working alongside us to achieve a higher level of productivity? That's the promise of Microsoft 365 Copilot, an innovative tool that uses the power of artificial intelligence to streamline our daily workflows. It's not about replacing human intelligence with technology but rather about enhancing our potential with it. This book is your roadmap to understanding and implementing this technology into your daily life. I will guide you through the concepts, teach you how to make the most out of them, and help you envision a work environment that is not only more efficient, but also more fulfilling.

It's time for us to change the way we work, to move beyond the limitations of our old ways. Microsoft 365 Copilot isn't just a tool; it's a partner that will reshape our work experience. This book will take you from the initial spark of curiosity to mastering the art of AI-driven productivity. Get ready to embark on this transformative journey and discover the power of AI to redefine your workday and amplify your overall impact.

The Rise of AI in Productivity Tools

History of Microsoft 365 and AI Integration

To truly appreciate the power of Microsoft 365 Copilot, we first need to understand where it all began. The history of Microsoft 365 and its journey into the world of AI is a story of innovation, persistence, and a vision for the future of work.

Microsoft's foray into office productivity software dates back to the early 1980s when the company introduced its first office tools. These early programs—Word, Excel, and PowerPoint—were revolutionary at the time, offering professionals a digital means to manage documents, data, and presentations. Back then, these tools were seen as game-changers. I remember my first interaction with Microsoft Word; it felt like magic compared to the clunky typewriters and handwritten notes we were used to. But as powerful as these early tools were, they required every ounce of our focus and effort. There was no automation, no shortcuts—just hours of manual labor.

Fast forward to the 1990s and early 2000s, Microsoft continued to refine its software offerings, but the real transformation came in the 2010s with the introduction of Office 365, a cloud-based version of their traditional office suite. This shift allowed users to access their documents from anywhere, collaborate in real time, and always have the latest version of the software. But while Office 365 made workflows more convenient, the real breakthrough came when Microsoft began to experiment with AI.

The journey into AI integration truly took off in 2016 with the introduction of features like "Smart Lookup" and "Tell Me" in Office 365, which gave users a taste of what AI could do. These tools helped users find information faster, but they were still quite basic compared to what was to come. Around this time, Microsoft began investing heavily in AI research, recognizing that the future of work would be shaped by intelligent systems capable of automating routine tasks and offering real-time insights.

By 2019, we started to see the fruits of this investment. Microsoft introduced AI-driven features like "Ideas" in Excel, which could suggest charts, identify trends, and even write formulas for you. For someone like me, who used to spend hours manually creating pivot tables and hunting for the right formula, these tools felt like a blessing. They saved time, reduced errors, and made data management more intuitive. But these were just the beginning.

In 2021, Microsoft made its most significant leap yet by announcing Microsoft 365 Copilot—a sophisticated AI assistant designed to help users navigate the complexities of modern office work. Copilot was not just an upgrade; it was a rethinking of how we interact with software. Built on the foundations of machine learning, natural language processing, and automation, Copilot promised to do more than simply answer questions or suggest templates. It aimed to learn from users, understand their habits, and proactively assist in ways that felt almost human.

The real power of Microsoft 365 Copilot lies in its ability to integrate deeply into the fabric of the Microsoft ecosystem. Whether you're drafting an email in Outlook, creating a report in Word, or analyzing data in Excel, Copilot is there, ready to assist. It can automate repetitive tasks, summarize documents, generate ideas, and even help you manage your schedule—all based on AI models that have been trained on vast amounts of data and user interactions.

Today, Microsoft 365 Copilot is at the forefront of AI-driven productivity tools, offering users the ability to work smarter, not harder. It's the culmination of decades of research and development, and it's clear that this is just the beginning. AI integration in office tools is poised to change the way we work forever.

When I think back to my early days of manually inputting data into spreadsheets, I can't help but marvel at how far we've come. What used to take hours of painstaking work can now be done in minutes with just a few clicks. Microsoft 365 Copilot is the epitome of this transformation—AI working seamlessly alongside us to make our work more efficient, accurate, and rewarding.

The path to Microsoft 365 Copilot wasn't a sprint; it was a marathon of strategic advancements and carefully orchestrated breakthroughs. Think of it like the construction of the Eiffel Tower, which wasn't achieved in a single leap but through multiple steps of planning, engineering, and implementation. Several key milestones marked this journey, each playing a critical role in shaping the AI-powered productivity tool we now have. One of the most crucial steps was the implementation of advanced natural language processing (NLP) capabilities. This technology allowed computers to understand and interpret human language with unprecedented accuracy, making it possible for users to interact with software in a more natural way, resembling the way we converse with each other rather than adhering to strict, coded commands. This was pivotal because it made the technology more user-friendly and accessible to a broader audience, removing the need for specialized skills or deep technical knowledge.

Another significant milestone was the development of machine learning algorithms capable of learning from vast amounts of data. This enabled the software to understand user habits, preferences, and patterns, allowing it to make more accurate and personalized recommendations and suggestions. It was akin to a seasoned chef who, having learned through years of experience, instinctively knows the right ingredients and techniques to create a perfect dish. By learning from each interaction, Microsoft 365 tools became more adaptive and intelligent, anticipating user needs and offering contextually relevant support. The development of sophisticated AI models for text and image analysis was another step, it meant that the technology was not only understanding words but also able to grasp the visual context of a document or a presentation, offering tools for enhanced content creation and editing. This wasn't just about speed; it was about enhancing quality and consistency.

The integration of AI into the cloud infrastructure was also crucial. This meant that AI-powered features could be delivered to users seamlessly, regardless of their location or device. It was a fundamental shift in how software is deployed and accessed, making cutting-edge technology available to a worldwide audience. Cloud computing also facilitated the continuous improvement of AI models, meaning that Microsoft 365 tools could benefit from the latest advancements without the need for any manual updates. Every one of these steps wasn't just about technology; it was about creating a user-centric experience. The milestones leading to Microsoft 365 Copilot represent a progression towards a more intuitive, adaptive, and personalized work environment. They showcase a journey of constant refinement and an unwavering focus on empowering users through the power of AI, leading to a tool that is ready to transform the way we work.

THE CONCEPT OF AI-POWERED PROMPTS

UNDERSTANDING PROMPTS: DEFINITION AND APPLICATION

At the heart of AI-driven tools like Microsoft 365 Copilot are prompts—simple yet powerful commands that allow you to communicate with AI in a way that feels intuitive. But what exactly are prompts, and how do they work within the context of productivity tools? To truly leverage the power of Microsoft 365 Copilot, it's essential to understand how prompts function, why they matter, and how they can be applied to supercharge your workflow.

Think of prompts as the instructions you give to the AI. Much like how you might ask a colleague for help, a prompt is a request for the AI to perform a specific action or provide a particular piece of information. The key difference, however, is that instead of explaining a task in detail, you only need to give a brief, clear command, and the AI handles the rest. It's a bit like having a virtual assistant who knows you well enough to anticipate what you need with just a few words.

For example, when using Microsoft 365 Copilot, you might input a prompt like, "Summarize this report." In a matter of seconds, Copilot will analyze the document, extract the key points, and present a concise summary. What used to take you hours—reading, highlighting, and drafting—now happens almost instantly. This is the magic of AI-powered prompts: they take the heavy lifting off your plate and give you more time to focus on decision-making and creative work.

Prompts aren't just for simple tasks like summarizing or searching, though. They can be incredibly versatile, allowing you to automate a wide range of processes across multiple Microsoft 365 applications. Need to generate an agenda for a meeting based on past correspondence? A simple prompt to Copilot will analyze your emails, pull out relevant topics, and create a structured agenda. Want to transform raw data into a well-formatted report? A single prompt can have Copilot sort, analyze, and present the data in an easily digestible format.

In practice, the use of prompts allows you to control AI in a way that feels both efficient and empowering. You don't need to be an expert in coding or even in the software you're using; all you need is the ability to communicate clearly. This simplicity is what makes AI-powered prompts such a game-changer, particularly for professionals who don't have time to learn complex systems or processes but need to get results quickly.

One of the best aspects of prompts is their adaptability. The more specific and refined your prompts are, the better the output you receive. For instance, if you're working on a presentation in PowerPoint and need a slide that highlights market trends, a prompt like "Create a slide showing the key market trends from the past year" will yield more targeted results than a vague "Make a slide about trends." Over time, as you become more familiar with how Copilot interprets prompts, you'll learn how to tailor your requests to get exactly what you need—saving time and ensuring accuracy.

Prompts also shine in collaborative environments. In tools like Microsoft Teams, you can use prompts to automate follow-ups, organize meeting notes, and even track the progress of group projects. Imagine having Copilot assist you by generating a project update based on the latest communications within your team—without you having to manually compile all the details. It's like having an extra team member whose sole purpose is to keep you organized and on track.

The concept of prompts might seem new, but it's actually rooted in something we've been doing for decades: issuing commands to our computers. From typing commands in early operating systems to using search engines or even voice assistants like Siri or Alexa, we've always interacted with technology by giving instructions. The difference with AI-powered prompts is that now the technology can understand and respond to much more complex, nuanced requests. Instead of simply executing a task, AI like Microsoft 365 Copilot interprets your command, processes the information, and delivers results that feel customized to your needs.

Understanding how prompts work is the first step to unlocking the full potential of Microsoft 365 Copilot. Once you grasp the basics of crafting effective prompts, the possibilities are endless. From managing your daily workload to automating time-consuming processes, prompts offer a level of efficiency that can transform the way you work. And the best part? You're in control. You tell the AI what you need, and it responds—not the other way around.

AI in Everyday Office Tasks

Now that we've established what prompts are, let's explore how they can be integrated into the routine of your daily work. Picture this as a skilled carpenter choosing the right tool for a specific task: they know that a saw isn't appropriate for driving nails, and likewise, we need to understand how to use the power of AI prompts to make our workflow more efficient. The beauty of AI prompts lies in their versatility. They aren't limited to a single type of task; they can be used across different applications and contexts. For instance, you might use a prompt to create a summary of a long email thread, turning a chaotic inbox into an organized view that allows you to quickly grasp the main points and make informed decisions. In another scenario, you could craft a prompt to create an outline for a presentation, and instead of starting from a blank canvas, you are now able to work from a structured framework, saving time and increasing the efficiency of your work. The key to using AI prompts in daily office tasks lies in recognizing the opportunities where they can add value and make the process smoother.

Let's talk about specific examples: Imagine you are preparing a report, and you could use a prompt to generate a first draft based on key data points you input, freeing you to dedicate more time to the analysis and refinement of this document, and saving you valuable time that can be better used for high-value activities. Or perhaps you are dealing with a complex dataset, and instead of manually searching through the information, a prompt could help you extract key insights and generate relevant charts that can be used directly in your report. Similarly, if you are managing multiple projects and finding it difficult to keep track of your tasks, you can use prompts to prioritize your workflow and generate reminders for upcoming deadlines. The idea is to think of AI as a partner, a tool that is always available to assist you in your daily tasks, a companion that can streamline your work and help you reach your objectives faster and more efficiently.

Beyond these concrete examples, consider the broader potential of AI prompts for tasks that require more creativity and innovation. You can use prompts to brainstorm new ideas, explore different perspectives, and develop innovative solutions. If you are developing marketing content, for instance, you can use a prompt to generate multiple variations of ad text, allowing you to test and refine your message, or if you are designing a new project, you can prompt the AI to generate alternative approaches and identify hidden opportunities. It's all about using prompts as a springboard for your creativity, helping you come up with ideas that you might not have considered using traditional approaches. The applications of AI in daily office tasks are as varied as your challenges. The key is to embrace a proactive approach, and instead of reacting to the challenges, to use prompts to address them head-on. By seeing these tools as partners, you can not only increase your productivity but also improve the overall quality of your work and unlock a higher degree of efficiency that you might not have believed possible. With the right approach, AI prompts will be the key to a more streamlined, innovative, and fulfilling work experience.

CHAPTER 1

1. BASICS OF MICROSOFT 365 COPILOT

To unlock the full potential of Microsoft 365 Copilot, it's important to start with the basics. Copilot isn't just another tool in your office suite—it's a transformative AI assistant that has the ability to understand your tasks, predict your needs, and deliver solutions tailored specifically to you. But before diving into advanced features, it's crucial to get familiar with how Copilot fits into the larger Microsoft 365 ecosystem.

At its core, Microsoft 365 Copilot is designed to help professionals work smarter, not harder. Imagine having an assistant that not only understands your workflow but also anticipates what you need before you even ask for it. Whether you're drafting emails, organizing data, or preparing a presentation, Copilot is there to take the mundane tasks off your hands, freeing you to focus on higher-level work. The great part is that Copilot integrates seamlessly with familiar Microsoft apps like Word, Excel, PowerPoint, Outlook, and Teams—tools you're likely using every day.

I remember when I first started exploring AI in my workflow—it felt like I had suddenly gained a personal assistant that could handle all the little things that usually ate up my time. No longer was I spending hours formatting documents or manually sorting through emails. Instead, I could focus on strategy, innovation, and the kind of creative work that had a real impact.

In this chapter, we'll take a closer look at how Microsoft 365 Copilot works, how to set it up, and how you can start using it immediately to boost your productivity. By the end of this chapter, you'll have a strong foundation in the basics of Copilot and be ready to dive deeper into more advanced features.

1.1. SETTING UP AND ACCESSING MICROSOFT 365 COPILOT

1.1.1. REQUIREMENTS AND INSTALLATION

Before you can experience the transformative power of Microsoft 365 Copilot, it is essential to make sure you have everything in place and that your system meets the requirements for its use. Think of this as preparing the foundation of a building. A solid and robust foundation will allow for a strong and resistant building. Similarly, in order to have the best experience with Copilot you need to make sure all the necessary steps are in place. The installation and setup process is designed to be user-friendly, even if you are not an experienced tech user. It's not as complex as it may seem, and I'll guide you step by step, making the process simple and stress-free. I always remember the first time I installed new software; the experience can be daunting, but following a few simple instructions made the whole process go much smoother, and here is how it is with Copilot.

First, you'll need to ensure that you have a Microsoft 365 subscription that includes Copilot. Not all subscriptions offer the same features, so it's essential to check your plan and make sure it includes this functionality. This is your first step, just like when you make sure you have all the ingredients to prepare a specific dish, and not all recipes can be created using the same basic ingredients. Once you have confirmed your subscription includes Copilot, you will proceed with the installation process, which will differ based on whether you are using a Windows, Mac, or other operating system. The process is not complicated, and is usually intuitive, but I will show you all the steps so that nothing is left behind. The idea is to make sure you are ready to make the most out of all the features of this new tool. You'll also want to make sure your applications are up to date, including Word, Excel, PowerPoint, Outlook, and Teams, because Copilot works seamlessly with these tools, and you won't have the best experience if you aren't using the latest versions. In addition to software, the hardware you are using will also make a difference, and you need to make sure that your machine has enough processing power and memory for Copilot to work as expected.

Once you have made sure all the software and hardware requirements are met, you are ready to proceed to the installation of Copilot, which is done within the Microsoft 365 ecosystem. I'll walk you through the process of enabling Copilot, as well as activating and setting up the tool. While the process is usually simple, I will explain each step in detail so you are able to implement these changes. The goal is to make sure that you can integrate Copilot into your daily workflow without any hassle. Once Copilot is enabled, it will be integrated with your existing tools, and you will be able to access it directly from the applications you use every day. Before starting your journey with Copilot, it's essential to make sure all the necessary steps are in place so you don't encounter any issues and you can use it to its full potential. By the time you finish setting everything up, you'll be ready to delve into its features and start using them to make your work more efficient and productive. This initial setup is crucial to your transformation, providing the base upon which you will build your AI-powered productivity skills.

1.1.2. BASIC NAVIGATION AND KEY FEATURES

Once you've installed and activated Microsoft 365 Copilot, it's time to dive into the core of the experience—learning how to navigate the platform and harness its most powerful features. The beauty of Copilot lies in its seamless integration with familiar Microsoft 365 apps, and getting comfortable with navigating these tools is key to unlocking your full productivity potential.

Navigating Microsoft 365 Copilot

Microsoft 365 Copilot is designed to blend into the tools you're already using, so you won't need to learn a whole new interface. You'll find Copilot embedded within Microsoft's major apps: Word, Excel, PowerPoint, Outlook, and Teams. The key difference is that Copilot introduces AI-driven assistance to your workflows, appearing as subtle prompts, suggestions, or even predictive features as you work.

In Word, for example, you'll notice Copilot in the form of a sidebar or small icon that suggests actions as you write. Need help organizing your thoughts? Copilot will offer to outline your document based on what you've already written. Are you struggling to find the right tone? Copilot might suggest alternative phrasing that's more concise or formal, depending on your audience.

In Excel, Copilot will live in the background, ready to assist with data analysis, formatting, and even advanced calculations. You can access Copilot suggestions through a sidebar or prompt it with commands like "Analyze this data" or "Create a forecast." For anyone who's ever struggled with complex formulas or data visualization, this feature is a game-changer.

In PowerPoint, Copilot's role becomes even more visual. It helps you create polished, professional presentations by suggesting layouts, formatting text, and even generating entire slides based on your input. With just a few clicks, you can turn raw data into a beautiful, cohesive presentation.

The key to navigating Microsoft 365 Copilot is simply knowing where to look. The AI is always working in the background, and its prompts are designed to appear when you need them most—whether it's summarizing a report in Word, generating charts in Excel, or drafting emails in Outlook.

Key Features of Microsoft 365 Copilot

Now that you've got a sense of where Copilot lives within the Microsoft ecosystem, let's explore some of its most powerful features. These are the tools that will save you time, improve your efficiency, and make your day-to-day tasks feel a lot less burdensome.

1. **AI-Generated Suggestions** One of the most valuable features of Copilot is its ability to offer real-time suggestions. As you work, Copilot will monitor your tasks and provide helpful prompts. In Word, for example, Copilot can suggest sentence rephrasings, offer grammar and style

improvements, or even help structure your writing. In Excel, it might suggest ways to clean up data, generate reports, or provide advanced formulas to solve complex problems.

These suggestions are more than just tips—they're actions you can accept or modify with a single click, streamlining your workflow without interrupting your focus.

2. **Task Automation** Automation is where Copilot truly shines. Routine tasks like organizing emails, scheduling meetings, or creating reports can be automated with just a few simple prompts. In Outlook, for example, you can use Copilot to automatically draft responses to frequently asked questions or even prioritize your inbox based on the urgency of messages. It's like having a personal assistant managing your email for you, so you don't have to waste time on repetitive communication. In Excel, Copilot can automate complex data processes. Whether it's building pivot tables, creating charts, or even analyzing trends, Copilot handles the heavy lifting so you can focus on interpreting the results.

3. **Smart Data Analysis** One of the most intimidating aspects of working with data is understanding how to analyze it effectively. This is where Copilot's AI really comes in handy. By leveraging machine learning models, Copilot can quickly analyze large datasets, identify trends, and even make predictions based on your historical data. For instance, if you're working on a sales report, you can prompt Copilot to "Identify sales trends for the last quarter," and it will generate a detailed analysis in minutes. It's like having a team of data

scientists at your fingertips, helping you make informed decisions without needing to be an expert in analytics.

4. **Collaboration Enhancement** In today's work environment, collaboration is key, and Microsoft 365 Copilot is designed to enhance this aspect of your workflow. In Microsoft Teams, Copilot can summarize meeting notes, track action items, and even follow up on tasks after a meeting ends. It keeps everyone on the same page, ensuring that no detail is overlooked and that projects move forward smoothly.

    Copilot also excels in document collaboration. If you're working with a team on a shared Word document, Copilot can track changes, suggest edits, and even ensure that the writing style is consistent throughout the document. It's like having an editor built into your workflow, making collaboration smoother and more efficient.

5. **Real-Time Learning and Adaptation** One of the most exciting features of Microsoft 365 Copilot is its ability to learn and adapt to your specific needs over time. The more you use Copilot, the better it understands your workflow and preferences. For example, if you frequently write formal emails, Copilot will begin to suggest formal language as you compose new messages. If you prefer certain styles of data visualization in Excel, Copilot will start offering those formats first.

    This learning process makes Copilot feel like a personalized assistant that's tailored to your unique work style. Over time, it will anticipate your needs, allowing you to work even more efficiently.

1.2. Using Microsoft 365 Copilot Across Applications

1.2.1. Copilot in Word, Excel, and PowerPoint

Let's focus first on how Microsoft 365 Copilot transforms your experience in **Word**, acting as a personal writing assistant, editor, and formatting expert, all within the familiar interface. Think of this as having a skilled writing partner always ready to collaborate with you, helping you to turn your ideas into clear, engaging, and polished documents. I will now provide concrete examples, guiding you through each step, so you can seamlessly integrate Copilot into your daily workflow and begin to unlock its transformative potential, taking advantage of its different features to create high-quality documents with greater efficiency and less effort.

Let's start with a common challenge: overcoming the initial blank page. If you need to write a report, a proposal, or even just a simple email, Copilot can provide a great starting point. Imagine you have to write a report about the impact of remote work on employee productivity. Instead of starting from scratch, you can use a prompt like, "Generate a 500-word report on the impact of remote work on employee productivity, including the benefits and challenges," and Copilot will generate a draft outline. This outline includes key points, suggestions for different sections, and even a basic introduction, saving you the time and effort of structuring your document from scratch. This provides you with a concrete starting point, helping you overcome that initial writing block and making it easier for you to focus on the content you want to produce. To start using Copilot effectively, open a Word document and locate the Copilot icon, typically found in the ribbon. Click on it to open the sidebar, where you can input your prompts and interact with AI. Once you have your prompt ready, simply type it into the text box and press "Enter," and Copilot will begin to work on your request.

But Copilot's assistance isn't limited to generating first drafts. Once you have content in place, you can use Copilot to revise and improve it. Let's say you have written a section of your document, but you want to make it more persuasive. You can select the text and use a prompt like, "Improve the tone of this paragraph to be more persuasive and engaging," and Copilot will analyze the tone, modify the vocabulary, and enhance the structure. If you have a long paragraph and you want to make it more concise, you can ask Copilot to, "Summarize this paragraph into three sentences," and the system will automatically identify the core points. This doesn't just save time; it enhances the overall quality of your text, making it more effective and impactful. Moreover, you can also use Copilot to check your documents for any grammatical errors. To do so, simply write: "Check this document for grammar and spelling errors and suggest corrections," and Copilot will review your entire text and highlight any mistakes, and then offer recommendations.

Copilot can also help you with formatting, ensuring your documents meet specific style guidelines. If you need to follow a specific style or template, you can use a prompt like, "Apply a professional style template to this document, using a 12-point Times New Roman font and double spacing," and Copilot will automatically apply the formatting across your entire document. This ensures uniformity and consistency across all your documents, enhancing their professional appearance. If you want to make specific changes to the formatting you can use a prompt like "Make all headings bold and use a 14-point font size," and Copilot will apply those changes in a matter of seconds. Copilot can also assist in converting your document into different formats. For instance, you can ask Copilot to, "Convert this document into PDF" or "Export it as a webpage," and it will prepare the file in the format you need. These features will not only increase your productivity but also ensure the consistency of your work, making Copilot an invaluable tool that is always ready to assist you. By using specific prompts to help with any aspect of your writing process, you can now transform your experience of working with Word, making it a seamless and creative process. Copilot isn't just an add-on tool; it's a partner that's ready to help you with your writing.

Let's now delve into how Microsoft 365 Copilot revolutionizes your work in **Excel**, transforming it from a complex spreadsheet tool into a powerful data analysis and insights engine. Think of this as having a skilled data analyst always at your disposal, simplifying complex data sets and turning them into actionable information. I will guide you through real-world examples and provide precise instructions, allowing you to integrate Copilot into your daily tasks and unlock the full potential of your spreadsheets, making your data analysis more efficient, accurate, and insightful.

Excel, often considered challenging and time-consuming, can now be navigated more easily using Copilot. To start using Copilot effectively, open your Excel workbook and look for the Copilot icon, usually located on the ribbon. Click on the icon to open the sidebar, which is where you input your prompts and receive AI assistance. Let's look at a common scenario: imagine you have a large sales dataset, and you need to identify the top-performing products from the last quarter, you can use a prompt like, "Analyze the sales data for the last three months and show the top-selling products," and Copilot will quickly identify the requested items. If you want to focus on a specific region you can use: "Analyze the sales data for the last three months and show the top-selling products, filtering by region: Northeast." From that, Copilot can generate a table or a chart, saving you the manual work. It also allows you to identify outliers in your data. You can use prompts like, "Identify any outliers in the sales data for the past year," and the system will point out any data entries that are significantly different from the rest, which is incredibly useful for quality control.

Copilot isn't only about simplifying data analysis; it also helps with complex formulas. Instead of spending hours searching for the correct function or typing out complicated equations, you can ask Copilot to create formulas for you. For example, if you need to calculate the average sales per customer, you can use a prompt like, "Create a formula to calculate the average sales per customer and apply it to the whole dataset," and Copilot will not only generate the formula but also apply it to your entire spreadsheet, saving you time and reducing the risk of errors. If you want to do a more advanced analysis you can use: "Create a formula to calculate the profit margin for each product, considering sales revenue, and cost," Copilot will not only create the formula but also apply it to your sheet, providing you with a complete breakdown. This is incredibly helpful if you have a large number of calculations and can save you hours of work.

Furthermore, Copilot can assist with data visualization, creating charts and graphs directly from your data. You can use prompts like: "Create a chart comparing the sales performance of each product category over the past year," and Copilot will generate a visually compelling chart that you can use in your reports or presentations, helping you communicate your findings with clarity. If you want to highlight specific aspects of your data you can use: "Create a pie chart visualizing the distribution of customers by region," and Copilot will instantly generate the graph for your data. Copilot makes data visualization more accessible, allowing you to generate clear and insightful visuals without having to spend hours mastering complex charting tools. Copilot also allows you to extract specific subsets from your data. For instance, you can use prompts like: "Filter the dataset to show only customers from the age group 25-35" or, "Filter the dataset to show all products with sales over 1000 units," Copilot will provide you with the relevant data you need in a matter of seconds. These prompts allow you to filter information, making your datasets easier to analyze. Copilot isn't just a tool; it's your AI-powered data analyst that will help you turn your spreadsheets into a powerhouse of insights.

Now, let's turn our focus to how Microsoft 365 Copilot enhances your experience with **PowerPoint**, transforming it from a basic presentation tool into a dynamic storytelling platform. Think of Copilot as your personal presentation designer, ready to help you craft visually stunning and impactful slides, ensuring your ideas are communicated effectively, with a design that enhances the message you are trying to convey. I will provide specific examples and clear instructions on how to integrate Copilot into your workflow, so you can immediately start using it to create presentations that not only capture the attention of your audience but also leave a lasting impact, making you more effective at communicating your ideas.

To start effectively using Copilot in PowerPoint, you should first open your presentation and find the Copilot icon, usually located in the ribbon, then click on the icon to open the sidebar. From there, you can input your prompts and interact with the AI. Let's look at a common challenge: creating a presentation from scratch. Instead of starting with a blank slide, you can use a prompt like, "Create a 10-slide presentation about the future of sustainable energy, including key trends and innovative solutions," and Copilot will generate an entire framework for you. This framework includes slide titles, key points, and even suggestions for relevant images, saving you considerable time and effort. This is not about having a system do all the work for you; it is about having a solid starting point that allows you to focus on the strategic and creative aspects of your presentation, allowing you to transform the way you approach your presentations. If you are working with a specific number of slides you can ask, "Create a 5-slide presentation about the benefits of Artificial Intelligence in Education" and Copilot will adjust accordingly.

Copilot also assists with content generation, so once you have your outline, you can ask Copilot to help you populate the slides with content. If you have a title for a specific slide you can ask Copilot to, "Generate a three-bullet point list for this slide about the main challenges of adopting AI in companies," and the system will provide you with accurate and concise content that will be ready for you to adjust to your needs. This isn't just about filling up slides; it's about providing content that is well-structured and well-written, ensuring your message is conveyed effectively. If you already have content in a slide, you can ask Copilot to, "Rewrite this paragraph to make it more concise and impactful," and the system will refine your text, making it more readable and engaging. Copilot also helps you select appropriate visual elements and images for your presentation. If you have a slide title, you can ask Copilot to, "Suggest an image or icon for this slide that represents technological innovation," and the system will provide relevant suggestions, enhancing the visual appeal of your presentation.

Additionally, Copilot can help you with design suggestions. If you have a slide you are not happy with you can ask Copilot to, "Suggest different design ideas for slide number 3," and Copilot will recommend different layouts and color schemes. To further improve your presentation you can use prompts like, "Apply a professional template to this presentation" or "Apply a consistent font style across all the slides," Copilot will ensure that your presentation has a cohesive and professional look. Copilot also helps you to create animations, and you can ask Copilot to, "Add transition effects to these slides," and it will create smooth and dynamic slide transitions. Copilot is more than just a tool; it's your AI-powered design assistant, making you more effective and efficient at designing great presentations that will captivate your audience. This is about empowering you to deliver memorable and impactful presentations, transforming the way you present your ideas, and enhancing your ability to communicate effectively with your audience.

1.2.2. Copilot in Outlook and Teams

While tools like Word, Excel, and PowerPoint are central to most professional tasks, the real hub of day-to-day communication and collaboration happens in Outlook and Teams. Managing emails, coordinating meetings, and collaborating with colleagues can consume significant time. This is where Microsoft 365 Copilot steps in, streamlining these interactions and making communication more efficient. Let's explore how Copilot integrates into Outlook and Teams to enhance your productivity.

Copilot in Microsoft Outlook

For many professionals, Outlook is the nerve center of their workday. It's where emails flow in, meetings are scheduled, and task lists are managed. But managing an inbox can quickly become overwhelming, especially when you're trying to stay on top of important conversations while sifting through less relevant emails. Copilot in Outlook is designed to reduce this burden by helping you manage, organize, and respond to emails more efficiently.

One of the standout features of Copilot in Outlook is its ability to prioritize your emails. With a simple prompt like, "Summarize my unread emails and highlight important ones," Copilot can scan your inbox, summarize key messages, and even flag important emails based on sender or content. This means you can focus on what really matters without wasting time manually sorting through your inbox.

Another time-saving feature is Copilot's ability to draft emails for you. Let's say you need to respond to several similar emails—something routine like meeting requests or client inquiries. You can prompt Copilot with, "Draft responses to these emails," and it will automatically create replies based on the context of the messages. You can quickly review, make any necessary tweaks, and send them off with just a few clicks.

Additionally, Copilot can help you schedule meetings more effectively. Instead of going back and forth trying to find a suitable time, Copilot can cross-reference your calendar with the schedules of your colleagues and suggest the best meeting time. For example, a prompt like, "Schedule a 30-minute meeting with John and Sarah next week" will have Copilot do the work of finding an available slot and sending the invites—no need for endless email chains.

For those who regularly work with attachments or large amounts of email correspondence, Copilot can also search through emails for relevant documents or information. A prompt like, "Find the contract attached to the email from last month with Client X," will have Copilot locate the file without you having to dig through your archives. This is especially helpful when working on long-term projects where email threads can become convoluted.

Copilot in Microsoft Teams

As much as Outlook handles email communications, Microsoft Teams is the central platform for collaboration in modern workplaces. Whether it's managing projects, hosting meetings, or sharing updates with your team, Teams is where the action happens. Copilot in Teams enhances your ability to stay on top of these interactions, turning chaotic collaboration into smooth, organized workflows.

One of the most useful features of Copilot in Teams is its ability to summarize conversations and meetings. After a long meeting, instead of relying on your notes or trying to remember everything discussed, you can prompt Copilot with, "Summarize key points from today's meeting." In seconds, you'll have a concise summary that captures important decisions, action items, and follow-ups. This is a game-changer for busy professionals who juggle multiple meetings and need a reliable way to track tasks.

Copilot also shines in tracking tasks and deadlines. Imagine you've just finished a meeting where several team members were assigned tasks. Instead of manually updating your to-do list, you can prompt Copilot with, "Track action items from today's meeting," and it will automatically create tasks, assign them to the relevant people, and even send reminders. This ensures that nothing falls through the cracks, and everyone stays accountable.

Another powerful use case for Copilot in Teams is enhancing communication within channels. In a busy team environment, threads can get lengthy, and it's easy to miss critical updates. Copilot can monitor conversations and highlight important messages. For instance, you might prompt, "What were the key updates in the marketing channel today?" and Copilot will sift through the conversation to deliver the most relevant information. This reduces the need to scroll through long threads, saving time and keeping you focused on what's important.

Collaboration on documents within Teams is also streamlined with Copilot. If you're working on a shared document, such as a proposal or report, Copilot can track changes, suggest edits, and even ensure that everyone's contributions are in sync. By using prompts like, "Summarize recent changes to the team document," you can get a quick overview of progress without having to manually compare versions or track edits yourself.

Lastly, Copilot helps with managing meeting logistics in Teams. For virtual meetings, setting agendas and following up with action items are crucial for staying organized. Copilot can automate much of this process. A prompt like, "Set an agenda for tomorrow's project update meeting" will result in a structured agenda based on previous meeting notes, email correspondence, or team discussions. After the meeting, you can follow up with, "Send a recap of today's meeting to the team," and Copilot will generate and distribute the summary.

2. USING PROMPTS FOR TASK AUTOMATION

Now that we've established the foundation by exploring how Copilot works across different applications, let's dive deeper into the core of its transformative power: task automation through the use of prompts. Think of this as shifting gears in a car, and while understanding the basics was essential, we're now moving to a more powerful and dynamic stage. This chapter will equip you with practical strategies for creating effective prompts, the key to unlocking Copilot's full potential, and I will guide you through each step, providing real-world examples that are immediately applicable to your daily work. This knowledge isn't just about learning how to use a tool; it's about transforming the way you approach your work, helping you to achieve a new level of efficiency.

We will explore the art of crafting prompts that yield precise results, which means understanding how AI interprets our requests and adjusting your phrasing accordingly. It will also help to think about prompts as more than simple commands, but rather as collaborative dialogues that help the AI become a partner in your daily tasks. This approach will be crucial to not only improve your productivity but also to enhance the quality of your work. This chapter will equip you with the skills you need to transform your workflow, from managing emails to creating reports, and will help you make Copilot a central tool in your everyday routine.

The aim of this chapter is to empower you to harness AI to its full extent, making Copilot not just a useful tool but rather an essential element that will allow you to reduce the burden of repetitive tasks and achieve more with less effort. This is about taking control of your work, and not just being a passive user of your software. You'll gain the skills to craft effective prompts, allowing you to integrate this powerful technology into your daily life, and making your approach to work more dynamic, more efficient, and more satisfying. So, get ready to dive into the practical aspects of AI-driven automation and see how you can use prompts to transform the way you work.

2.1. CRAFTING EFFECTIVE PROMPTS

2.1.1. HOW AI INTERPRETS PROMPTS

Crafting effective prompts is both an art and a science. When working with AI-powered tools like Microsoft 365 Copilot, the clearer your prompt, the better the results you'll get. Understanding how AI interprets these prompts is essential to unlocking the full potential of automation. Think of prompts as conversations with your AI assistant—the more precise and direct you are, the more accurately it can assist you.

At its core, AI interprets prompts based on natural language processing (NLP), which allows it to understand human language in a way that feels intuitive. But unlike a human assistant, who might infer meaning from context or read between the lines, AI requires clarity and specificity. This doesn't mean you need to be robotic or overly formal—just purposeful and concise in your requests.

For example, imagine you're working on a quarterly report and you need to analyze sales data. A vague prompt like, "Look at the sales numbers," might lead to a response that's too broad or not actionable. Instead, a more effective prompt would be something like, "Analyze the sales data from Q3 and provide a summary of the top-performing products." By specifying the time frame (Q3), the data set (sales data), and the desired output (a summary of top-performing products), you're giving Copilot all the information it needs to deliver exactly what you want.

One of the most powerful aspects of AI, particularly within Microsoft 365 Copilot, is its ability to learn from your interactions. The more you use it, the more familiar it becomes with your preferences, tasks, and the nuances of your requests. However, AI still operates within the parameters of the instructions you provide, which is why crafting effective prompts is critical.

Let's take another example from a different tool—Microsoft Word. Suppose you're drafting a document and you want Copilot to help you improve the tone and flow. A basic prompt like, "Make this better," won't be very helpful. Instead, try something more specific, such as, "Rephrase this paragraph to sound more formal and concise." Now, Copilot understands not only that you want changes, but exactly how you want them—formal and concise. The more information you give, the more tailored the AI's response will be.

Another key factor to keep in mind is that AI operates on logic. This means that if your request isn't clear or leaves too much ambiguity, the AI may not produce the result you're looking for. It's a little like giving directions—if you just say "Take me somewhere nice," the result could be anything from a beach to a coffee shop. But if you say, "Take me to a quiet beach where I can relax," you'll likely end up where you actually want to be.

When it comes to complex tasks, breaking down your prompt into smaller steps can be incredibly useful. Let's say you're working in Excel, and you need Copilot to generate a report based on a large dataset. Instead of prompting, "Generate a sales report," you could break it down into more manageable parts: "Organize the sales data by region," followed by, "Identify the top-selling product in each region," and finally, "Create a summary report based on these findings." By structuring your prompts step-by-step, you give the AI a clear path to follow, ensuring more accurate and useful results.

It's also worth noting that AI has its limits. While Microsoft 365 Copilot is incredibly advanced, it's not yet capable of reading your mind or making decisions for you. It relies on the input you provide to shape its output. So, if you find that Copilot isn't quite delivering the results you were hoping for, take a step back and examine your prompts. Are they specific? Are they clear? Are you giving enough detail for the AI to fully understand your request?

Over time, as you become more familiar with how Copilot interprets prompts, you'll get better at refining your instructions. You'll learn what works and what doesn't, and you'll start to see patterns in the way the AI responds. This process of learning and refining is key to making the most of AI-powered tools in your daily workflow.

One analogy I often use is that crafting prompts for AI is like teaching someone a new skill. At first, you need to give clear, step-by-step instructions. But as the person (or AI) becomes more familiar with the task, they start to understand your expectations and can perform more complex tasks with less guidance. It's a learning process on both sides.

By the end of this section, you'll have a deeper understanding of how Microsoft 365 Copilot interprets prompts, and you'll be well-equipped to craft instructions that lead to precise, valuable outcomes. The more intentional you are with your prompts, the more powerful your AI assistant will become.

2.1.2. BEST PRACTICES FOR WRITING PROMPTS

Writing effective prompts is one of the key skills you'll need to master in order to unlock the full potential of Microsoft 365 Copilot. While Copilot is designed to understand natural language, there are best practices you can follow to make sure your prompts yield the most accurate and useful results. The clearer and more specific you are in your requests, the more efficiently the AI can assist you.

Be Specific and Clear

The first and most important rule for writing effective prompts is clarity. The more detailed and specific your instructions, the better Copilot can understand what you want. Let's take an example: if you're working in Excel and you need help analyzing sales data, a vague prompt like, "Help with sales data," will likely produce a response that's too broad. Instead, a more effective prompt would be, "Analyze Q2 sales data and provide a summary of the top-performing products by region." This gives Copilot a clear direction: which data to analyze (Q2 sales), what to focus on (top-performing products), and how to structure the output (by region).

When crafting prompts, think about the key pieces of information the AI will need to deliver an accurate result. Ask yourself:

- What specific task do I need help with?
- What data or content should the AI focus on?
- What format do I want the output to be in?

By including these elements in your prompts, you help the AI avoid ambiguity and deliver exactly what you're looking for.

Break Down Complex Tasks

If you're dealing with a large or multi-step process, it can be helpful to break down your request into smaller, more manageable prompts. For instance, let's say you're working on a project report in Word. Instead of asking Copilot to "Create a full project report," you could break the task into stages:

1. "Create an outline for the project report."
2. "Draft the introduction based on last month's meeting notes."
3. "Summarize the key deliverables from the project timeline."

By breaking down the task, you guide Copilot through the process in a logical sequence. This not only ensures that each step is handled carefully but also makes it easier to review and adjust the output as you go.

Use Actionable Language

When writing prompts, use actionable verbs that clearly indicate what you want the AI to do. Words like "summarize," "generate," "analyze," "draft," and "organize" tell Copilot exactly what kind of task to perform. For example, a prompt like, "Summarize the key takeaways from this email thread," gives Copilot a direct instruction, whereas a less specific request like, "What's important in this email?" may lead to less useful results.

Actionable language helps the AI focus on the task at hand, minimizing any misinterpretation of your request.

Provide Context Where Needed

Context is essential for helping Copilot understand the bigger picture of your request. If you're asking for a summary, for example, make sure to specify what context you're working in. Imagine you're using Word to draft a business proposal. You might prompt, "Summarize this document for a client meeting." By including the context of a client meeting, Copilot understands that the summary should focus on key points that are relevant for external communication, rather than internal team details.

Similarly, if you're using Excel and want Copilot to forecast sales, provide context on the timeframe and data source: "Create a sales forecast for the next quarter based on the

Q2 sales data." The more context you provide, the more tailored and accurate the output will be.

Refine as You Go

One of the great things about working with Copilot is that you can refine your prompts as needed. If the initial output isn't exactly what you were looking for, don't hesitate to revise your prompt and try again. For instance, if you asked Copilot to "Generate a slide summarizing sales trends" and the result wasn't detailed enough, you can refine your prompt: "Generate a slide summarizing sales trends over the last six months, including regional breakdowns and product performance."

By iterating and refining your prompts, you can guide Copilot towards more precise results. Over time, you'll develop a sense of how much detail is needed and what types of requests work best.

Be Open to Suggestions

While clarity is important, it's also a good idea to leave some room for Copilot's suggestions. Sometimes, the AI can offer insights or solutions that you hadn't considered. For example, if you're unsure how to structure a document, you could prompt, "Draft an outline for a business proposal," and let Copilot suggest a structure based on best practices. This is especially useful in situations where you might not have a clear starting point, as Copilot can help you organize your ideas and generate new approaches.

Practice and Experiment

Like any skill, crafting effective prompts takes practice. The more you work with Copilot, the better you'll get at phrasing your requests in a way that produces the best outcomes. Don't be afraid to experiment with different approaches to see how Copilot responds. Try varying the level of detail, rephrasing instructions, or giving more creative prompts. This experimentation can help you uncover new ways to use the AI that you might not have thought of before.

For example, in Teams, you might start with a prompt like, "Summarize today's meeting," but as you get more comfortable with the tool, you could expand your requests to, "Summarize the meeting and create a task list from the action items discussed." By pushing the boundaries of what you ask Copilot to do, you'll discover even more ways it can streamline your work.

By following these best practices for writing prompts, you'll not only improve the accuracy of Copilot's responses but also unlock its full potential to enhance your productivity. Crafting clear, specific, and actionable prompts is the key to making the most of Microsoft 365 Copilot, whether you're drafting documents, analyzing data, or managing communications.

2.2. AUTOMATING COMMON OFFICE TASKS

2.2.1. AUTOMATING EMAIL MANAGEMENT

Let's now focus on how you can use prompts to automate common office tasks, starting with a critical area for many professionals: email management. Think of this as streamlining a busy factory line, where each step is carefully optimized for maximum efficiency, and repetitive manual actions are replaced with intelligent automated processes. For many of us, email inboxes can quickly become overwhelming, filled with messages that demand immediate attention. This is where Copilot comes in, transforming your approach to email management and helping you to save time, stay organized, and focus on what really matters. I will guide you through the various steps, providing real-world examples and actionable tips you can use to immediately integrate AI into your daily email routines, and allowing you to free up valuable time for more strategic and creative activities.

One of the most powerful applications of Copilot for email management is its ability to summarize long email threads. Imagine you've returned from vacation, and you are faced with an inbox full of messages, many of which are long and complex conversations. Instead of trying to read through every message to catch up, you can use a prompt like, "Summarize this email thread, and provide a list of key decisions," and Copilot will quickly provide a concise overview of the entire conversation, listing the main action items, and saving you a significant amount of time. To use this feature, simply select the email thread you want to summarize, open Copilot, and input the prompt in the chat bar, and Copilot will quickly analyze the entire thread and produce a summary. If you need to refine your request, you can add more detail, such as: "Summarize this email thread, highlighting the action items assigned to me with deadlines," and Copilot will provide a customized summary, focusing on the specific information you are looking for. This feature not only saves time but also helps you to stay informed and organized.

Copilot is also incredibly effective at drafting email responses, helping you compose messages quickly and professionally. Imagine you need to respond to a client inquiry, but you are short on time, you can use a prompt like, "Draft a professional response to this inquiry, including a summary of our services and pricing," and Copilot will provide a tailored draft. You can ask the system to, "Draft a polite email declining the offer, but expressing gratitude for the opportunity," and it will generate an email that meets your requirements. By using prompts, you can create clear and professional messages in a fraction of the time it would normally take. This functionality isn't about replacing your communication skills; it's about enhancing them, helping you to convey your message more efficiently. To use this feature, simply open the email you want to reply to, open Copilot, type in the prompt, and Copilot will generate a draft. If you want to adjust the tone of the generated message you can ask Copilot to, "Adjust the tone of this email to be more formal," and it will make the corresponding adjustments to the text. You can also use it to shorten your message: "Summarize this email to be less than 100 words," and Copilot will adapt to your instructions.

Another significant aspect of Copilot in email management is its ability to prioritize your inbox. Instead of manually sorting through your emails, you can use prompts to identify the most important messages. You can ask Copilot to, "List the emails from my manager and highlight the urgent ones," or, "List the emails with the subject 'Project Update' and group them by sender," and Copilot will organize your inbox based on your parameters. You can also use prompts to filter and organize emails by keywords. For example, if you want to find all emails relating to a specific project you can ask Copilot to, "Filter all emails containing the word 'Project Alpha' and move them to the folder 'Project Alpha'." Copilot also helps you to categorize emails more efficiently, automatically moving them into the right folders, and streamlining your workflow. You can ask Copilot to "Move all emails from the 'Marketing' department to the folder 'Marketing communications'", or, "Create a folder called 'Customer Feedback' and move all emails with the subject 'Customer Review'," and Copilot will make those changes in your inbox. By automating these sorting tasks you are able to keep your inbox clean and organized, freeing you from the burden of these repetitive tasks.

Furthermore, Copilot helps you schedule meetings and appointments by extracting key information directly from your emails, eliminating the need to manually extract these details. If you receive an email proposing a meeting you can use a prompt like, "Schedule a meeting based on the information in this email and send an invitation to all the participants," and Copilot will automatically populate your calendar with the required details. You can also ask Copilot to, "Find the next available time slot in my calendar and propose it as a meeting time for this meeting," and Copilot will automatically verify your calendar and propose an available slot, streamlining your meeting scheduling process. Finally, Copilot can assist you with setting reminders and task lists based on your email content. If you have an action item mentioned in an email, you can ask Copilot to: "Create a task in my list based on this email, setting the deadline to next Friday," and Copilot will automatically create a task in your Microsoft To-Do list, saving you time and helping you stay on track of your pending tasks.

2.2.2. Automating Document Creation and Editing

Document creation and editing can be some of the most time-consuming tasks in a professional environment. Whether you're drafting reports, preparing client proposals, or revising important contracts, the process often requires significant attention to detail, careful wording, and multiple rounds of edits. Microsoft 365 Copilot streamlines this process by using AI to automate document creation and editing, allowing you to focus more on the content and strategy while the AI handles the mechanics.

Drafting Documents with Copilot

Imagine you've been tasked with writing a detailed project proposal for an upcoming client meeting. In the past, you might have spent hours drafting the initial version, researching the content, and organizing your thoughts. With Copilot, you can significantly reduce the time spent on these tasks. A simple prompt like, "Draft a project proposal based on our previous meeting notes," allows Copilot to pull the relevant information from your documents and emails, generating an organized draft in minutes.

Copilot is especially useful when it comes to working with templates. If your company has standard templates for reports, proposals, or contracts, you can use prompts to quickly populate those templates with the necessary information. For example, a prompt like, "Fill in the project template with the client's details and deliverables," will automatically input the relevant information, leaving you with a nearly finished document that requires minimal additional editing.

The AI's ability to adapt to different tones and formats is another strength. If you're drafting a document for internal use, you might want a more informal tone. For external clients, a more formal and polished style is required. Copilot can adapt to these needs based on your instructions. You could prompt, "Draft a client proposal using a formal tone," and Copilot will adjust the language to match the context.

Enhancing Writing and Clarity

Once your document is drafted, Copilot's editing features take over. Editing is often the most tedious part of the writing process—fine-tuning the wording, checking for grammar mistakes, and ensuring the content flows logically. Copilot makes this process easier by offering suggestions for improvement as you write or edit.

For example, if a paragraph in your report feels too long or confusing, you can prompt Copilot with, "Rewrite this paragraph to make it clearer and more concise." Copilot will analyze the text and suggest a reworded version that improves clarity and readability. It can also help with tone and style adjustments. A prompt like, "Make this section sound more professional," will result in a revised version that better suits formal business communication.

Copilot also assists with grammar and spell-checking, much like traditional tools, but with more sophistication. Instead of just identifying errors, it offers suggestions for rephrasing sentences to improve overall flow and readability. For professionals who often find themselves racing against deadlines, this feature is a lifesaver, providing quick, accurate edits without the need for extensive proofreading.

Collaborating on Documents

Another area where Copilot shines is in document collaboration. Working with colleagues on shared documents can sometimes feel chaotic—multiple versions, overlapping edits, and conflicting feedback can make the process cumbersome. Copilot smooths out these issues by keeping track of changes, summarizing edits, and ensuring that everyone is working from the most up-to-date version of the document.

Let's say you're working on a joint report with several team members. Instead of manually reviewing each person's contributions, you can prompt Copilot to, "Summarize the recent changes made by the team." This prompt will give you a quick overview of who edited what, allowing you to focus on the big picture without getting bogged down in the details.

Copilot also facilitates easier communication around edits. If a colleague leaves comments in the document, you can use a prompt like, "Respond to the comments in this document," and Copilot will generate draft responses based on the feedback provided. This is particularly helpful in long documents where managing comments and revisions can become overwhelming.

Formatting and Finalizing Documents

Formatting a document can often take just as long as writing it, especially if you're dealing with specific formatting requirements for reports or presentations.

Copilot automates much of the formatting process, allowing you to focus on the content itself. With prompts like, "Format this report using our company's standard template," Copilot can apply styles, headings, bullet points, and even insert tables or charts based on the data provided.

In PowerPoint, Copilot takes formatting even further by helping you generate visually appealing slides from your text-based content. A prompt like, "Create slides based on this report," will result in a fully formatted presentation, complete with suggested layouts and graphics. This takes the headache out of creating slides manually, especially when you're pressed for time.

For Word documents, Copilot can also assist with adding references, footnotes, and even automating the table of contents. A prompt like, "Insert a table of contents based on the document's headings," will automatically generate a clean, professional table of contents that updates dynamically as you edit the document.

Editing for Specific Audiences

One of the unique aspects of Copilot's AI capabilities is its ability to tailor documents for different audiences. If you need to revise a report for different stakeholders—such as internal teams, clients, or senior management—you can prompt Copilot to adapt the document's tone and focus accordingly. For instance, "Revise this report for a technical audience," will result in a version that emphasizes data and technical details, whereas a prompt like, "Summarize this for an executive audience," will yield a more high-level overview with less focus on the granular details.

This ability to quickly pivot and adjust a document for multiple audiences ensures that you're always communicating effectively without having to start from scratch each time.

By automating document creation and editing with Microsoft 365 Copilot, you can significantly reduce the time spent on these tasks, allowing you to focus on higher-level thinking and strategy. Whether you're drafting from scratch, editing for clarity, or collaborating with a team, Copilot ensures that your documents are professional, polished, and ready to go with minimal effort on your part.

Chapter 3

3. Enhancing Workflow with AI

Having explored how AI can automate individual tasks, let's now shift our focus to the bigger picture: enhancing workflows with AI. Think of this as moving from optimizing individual tools to optimizing the entire workshop, where each process is seamlessly integrated to achieve greater efficiency. This chapter will guide you through how AI can optimize complex workflows, making team collaboration more effective and streamlining the way your organization operates. I will provide real-world examples, offering practical strategies you can implement to achieve significant improvements in the way you approach your work, empowering you to transform your organizational processes and achieve greater results.

We will explore how AI can improve project management, streamline team communication, and automate essential tasks, providing you with tools that not only make your work easier but also allow you to reach higher goals. This chapter will move from individual actions to a systematic approach, showing you how you can use AI to create a more fluid, integrated, and efficient organization. I will present concrete examples, providing clear instructions on how you can use Copilot in team settings to improve your overall results.

This is about taking advantage of technology to make your work more efficient, your collaboration more effective, and your results more impressive. This chapter aims to provide you with the knowledge and skills to transform the way your team works, using AI as a partner that will empower you to achieve more with less effort. By the end of this chapter, you'll be equipped to envision a new way of working, ready to use AI to elevate your entire organization.

3.1. WORKFLOW AUTOMATION WITH COPILOT

3.1.1. STREAMLINING REPORTS AND DATA ANALYSIS

One of the most time-consuming aspects of professional life is gathering, analyzing, and presenting data in the form of reports. Whether you're working on a quarterly financial report, tracking project milestones, or analyzing customer data, these tasks often require not only precision but also hours of manual work. Microsoft 365 Copilot changes this dynamic by streamlining the process of generating reports and analyzing data, allowing you to focus on insights rather than the mechanics of data handling.

Automating Data Collection and Organization

The first challenge of report generation often lies in collecting and organizing the data. Copilot automates this process by pulling relevant data from your documents, emails, spreadsheets, and databases. Imagine you're tasked with preparing a quarterly sales report. Instead of manually gathering figures from various Excel sheets or Salesforce reports, you can prompt Copilot with, "Generate a report on Q3 sales performance, including top-performing products by region." Copilot will sift through your data sources, organize the information, and deliver a structured report.

This automated data collection isn't just about saving time; it's about reducing errors. Manual data entry can lead to mistakes, especially when dealing with large datasets or repetitive tasks. Copilot minimizes this risk by automatically pulling accurate data and formatting it according to your needs. The end result is a cleaner, more reliable dataset that's ready for analysis.

Analyzing Data with Copilot

Once the data is collected, the next step is making sense of it. Traditionally, this would require you to spend time analyzing trends, identifying patterns, and creating visualizations to communicate your findings. Copilot simplifies this process by using AI to perform much of the analysis for you. A prompt like, "Analyze the Q3 sales data and highlight key trends," will have Copilot comb through the data, identifying patterns such as regional performance, product sales trends, or customer behavior changes.

This is where Copilot's true power lies—its ability to handle complex data analysis tasks in a fraction of the time it would take manually. Need to forecast future sales based on past performance? Just prompt Copilot with, "Create a sales forecast for Q4 based on historical trends," and you'll receive a projection that's backed by the data you've already collected.

Beyond numbers, Copilot can help you draw insights from qualitative data as well. If you've been tracking customer feedback or employee comments, for example, Copilot can analyze this information and provide summaries or sentiment analysis. A prompt like, "Summarize customer feedback from Q3 and identify common complaints," will give you an overview of the most pressing issues, allowing you to make data-driven decisions without getting lost in individual comments.

Generating Visual Reports

Visualizing data is a key component of any report, and Copilot excels in this area as well. Once your data has been analyzed, Copilot can automatically generate charts, graphs, and other visualizations that make your findings easy to understand and present. Let's say you need to present your sales data in a meeting. A prompt like, "Create a bar chart comparing Q3 sales by region," will result in a clear, visually appealing chart ready to be added to your report or presentation.

Copilot also makes it easy to update reports with new data. Instead of recreating charts and graphs every time you receive updated figures, you can simply prompt, "Update the sales report with the latest data from last week," and Copilot will refresh the visualizations and incorporate the new information seamlessly.

Customizing Reports for Different Audiences

One of the most powerful features of Copilot is its ability to customize reports based on the needs of different audiences. If you're creating a detailed financial report for internal stakeholders, you might need in-depth charts, tables, and explanations. But if you're summarizing the same data for a client or senior executive, you'll likely need a higher-level overview that focuses on key insights rather than technical details.

With Copilot, you can generate multiple versions of the same report, tailored to different audiences. For example, you could prompt, "Create an executive summary of the Q3 sales report for senior management," and Copilot will condense the data into a format that highlights the most important points without overwhelming the reader with details. On the other hand, a prompt like, "Generate a detailed financial report for the finance team," will provide all the granular data and analysis needed for internal review.

This ability to shift between high-level summaries and detailed reports ensures that you're always communicating the right information to the right audience, without having to start from scratch each time.

Reducing the Time Spent on Reports

By automating the data collection, analysis, and visualization processes, Copilot dramatically reduces the amount of time you spend generating reports. What used to take hours—or even days—can now be accomplished in minutes with just a few prompts. This frees you up to focus on interpreting the data and making strategic decisions based on the insights Copilot provides.

I remember when I used to dread report season. The sheer amount of manual work—gathering data, double-checking numbers, creating charts, formatting the document—felt overwhelming. But with Copilot, the entire process has been streamlined. Now, I can generate accurate, professional reports with minimal effort, allowing me to focus on the bigger picture and make informed decisions more quickly.

Enhancing Collaboration on Reports

In team settings, Copilot also facilitates easier collaboration on reports. If multiple people are contributing to a report, Copilot can track changes, summarize team contributions, and ensure that everyone is working from the same data set. A prompt like, "Summarize the changes made to the sales report by the team this week," gives you a clear view of what's been added or adjusted, so you can stay on top of the project without getting bogged down in version control issues.

With Copilot's AI-powered assistance, report generation and data analysis no longer have to be time-consuming, manual processes. By automating these tasks, Copilot enables you to focus on the insights that matter most, ensuring that your reports are not only accurate but also impactful. The result is a more efficient workflow, where you can spend less time on data handling and more time on driving results.

3.1.2. MANAGING PROJECT TIMELINES AND RESOURCES

Let's explore how Copilot can transform your approach to managing project timelines and resources, turning the complexities of project management into a streamlined and efficient process. Think of this as having a project management expert at your fingertips, always ready to assist you in planning, tracking, and optimizing your projects. By using Copilot effectively, you will not only be able to save time, but also improve the overall success of your projects by ensuring they are delivered on time and within budget. I will guide you through practical examples, showing you how to integrate AI into your project management routines, empowering you to achieve greater results with less effort.

One of the most valuable aspects of Copilot for project management is its ability to create realistic project timelines. Imagine you're starting a new project, and instead of manually trying to estimate timelines and dependencies, you can use a prompt like, "Create a detailed project timeline for the launch of a new product, including key milestones, task dependencies, and realistic deadlines," and Copilot will generate a complete timeline that you can adapt to your specific needs. If you want to focus on a specific aspect of the project you can ask Copilot to, "Create a detailed project timeline for the marketing phase of a new product, including key tasks, responsible team members, and deadlines." Copilot allows you to identify bottlenecks in the plan, and creates a timeline that is not only comprehensive but also realistic, saving you the headache of potential delays.

Copilot also helps with resource allocation, ensuring you have the right people and tools in place at the right time. Instead of manually trying to allocate team members to different project tasks, you can use a prompt like, "Analyze the project tasks and allocate team members based on their skills and availability," and Copilot will generate a resource allocation plan that you can adapt to your requirements. If you want to focus on a specific area you can ask Copilot to, "Allocate team members to the marketing tasks of this project, taking into account their past experience," and the AI will make these adjustments, making resource allocation more efficient. This feature ensures that all your team members are efficiently assigned to the tasks that best suit their skills, which increases productivity and minimizes the risk of delays or overspending.

Moreover, Copilot helps you to track project progress, and ensures that all tasks are on schedule. Imagine you want to quickly identify which tasks are at risk and what action is needed. You can use a prompt like, "Generate a report that shows all the tasks that are behind schedule and list the reasons for these delays," and Copilot will automatically identify the tasks that need your attention, and help you implement a mitigation strategy. If you want to focus on a specific aspect of the project you can ask Copilot to, "Create a project progress report, focusing on the tasks assigned to the marketing team, highlighting any potential delays," and the AI will provide a concise overview with key points that require your attention. This feature allows you to stay informed about all the progress of the project and to address potential issues before they impact the entire timeline.

Furthermore, Copilot helps you to manage project changes effectively, making it easier to adapt to unexpected circumstances. If you need to modify the project timeline you can use prompts like: "Adjust the project timeline due to the delay in the delivery of materials, highlighting all the changes in tasks and deadlines," and Copilot will modify the timeline in order to accommodate these changes and provide a list of the new deadlines. If you need to reallocate resources you can use prompts like: "Reallocate resources due to changes in the project scope, taking into account the new task priorities and team member's expertise," Copilot will modify your allocation plan and ensure that your project stays on track, allowing you to quickly adapt to unforeseen circumstances. This functionality not only saves you time but also makes your entire project more flexible and resilient. Finally, Copilot helps you communicate project updates to your stakeholders. You can use prompts like, "Generate a project progress report, summarizing the key milestones achieved, the current status, and any upcoming deadlines, for the stakeholders," and Copilot will automatically generate a report that you can share with your audience, keeping them informed about all the key aspects of the project, allowing you to communicate more effectively with all the stakeholders involved.

3.2. AI-Enhanced Collaboration

3.2.1. Boosting Team Communication in Microsoft Teams

Managing project timelines and resources is often one of the most challenging aspects of professional life. Balancing deadlines, tracking progress, and allocating resources effectively can feel like spinning plates—one misstep, and the whole system might come crashing down. Microsoft 365 Copilot helps streamline project management, allowing you to automate much of the administrative burden and keep projects running smoothly from start to finish.

Tracking Project Timelines with Copilot

One of the first hurdles in managing any project is ensuring that all tasks stay on track and that deadlines are met. Traditionally, this might require you to constantly check project management software, send follow-up emails, or manually update timelines as tasks progress. With Copilot, these processes can be automated, giving you real-time updates on project timelines with minimal effort.

Imagine you're overseeing a large project with multiple team members and overlapping deadlines. Instead of manually tracking each person's progress, you can prompt Copilot with, "Provide a status update on the project timeline," and it will automatically gather information from your project management tools, emails, and shared documents to give you a comprehensive overview of where things stand. If any tasks are behind schedule, Copilot can flag them and suggest ways to bring the project back on track.

Additionally, Copilot can automate the creation and updating of Gantt charts or other visual timelines. For example, you might ask, "Generate a Gantt chart for the product launch timeline," and Copilot will create a clear, visual representation of the project's stages, deadlines, and dependencies. These charts are invaluable for team meetings, helping everyone stay aligned and aware of key milestones.

Automating Task Assignments

One of the most tedious parts of managing a project is assigning tasks to team members, especially in large or complex projects with many moving parts. With Copilot, you can automate task assignments based on the skills, availability, and workload of your team members. For example, you might prompt, "Assign tasks for the upcoming sprint based on team availability," and Copilot will distribute the workload in a way that ensures no one is overwhelmed, and all tasks are covered.

This automation also allows you to reassign tasks quickly if someone is out of office or overloaded. A prompt like, "Reassign Sarah's tasks for this week to other team members," ensures that nothing falls through the cracks and that the project keeps moving forward, even if key personnel are unavailable.

Copilot can also track task completion, prompting follow-ups when necessary. If a task is overdue, Copilot can automatically send reminders to the responsible team members, ensuring that deadlines are met without you having to manually chase updates. A prompt such as, "Remind John to submit the draft by Friday," sets this process in motion, taking the administrative burden off your shoulders.

Optimizing Resource Allocation

Managing resources effectively is a critical part of project management, whether those resources are team members' time, budgets, or physical assets. Copilot helps streamline resource allocation by analyzing current workloads and making data-driven suggestions for optimizing efficiency.

For instance, if you're managing a marketing campaign and need to ensure that the team's workload is balanced, you can prompt, "Analyze team workload and suggest resource reallocation." Copilot will review the assigned tasks and identify any team members who are overburdened or underutilized, allowing you to redistribute tasks accordingly. This ensures that no one is overwhelmed, and everyone is contributing effectively to the project's success.

Additionally, Copilot can track your budget and resources over time, sending you updates and alerts if you're approaching resource limits. If you're nearing the end of a project and are running low on resources, Copilot might suggest re-prioritizing certain tasks or reallocating funds to ensure that the most critical parts of the project are completed on time and within budget. A prompt like, "Analyze current project budget and recommend adjustments," allows Copilot to provide actionable insights based on real-time data.

Managing Dependencies and Milestones

In complex projects, it's easy for teams to lose sight of dependencies between tasks. A delay in one area can have a cascading effect, throwing off the entire timeline. Copilot helps you manage these dependencies by tracking them and flagging any potential bottlenecks.

For example, if a report from one department is needed before another team can begin their work, Copilot will highlight this dependency and ensure that everyone involved is aware of the critical path. A prompt such as, "Identify task dependencies in the project timeline," will provide a clear map of where tasks overlap and which ones need to be completed first.

Milestones are another key element of project management, and Copilot makes it easy to track progress toward these important markers. You can prompt Copilot with, "Summarize progress toward project milestones," and it will generate a report that shows which milestones have been achieved, which ones are coming up, and any potential delays that need to be addressed. This allows you to proactively manage the project, ensuring that it stays on schedule.

Collaborating on Project Timelines and Resources

Copilot also makes collaboration on project timelines and resources more efficient. If you're working with a large team, you can use Copilot to keep everyone on the same page by automating updates and ensuring that changes to the timeline or resource allocation are communicated clearly.

For example, you might prompt, "Send a project update to the team highlighting changes to the timeline," and Copilot will generate a clear, concise update that summarizes the most recent developments and their impact on the overall project. This reduces the need for lengthy meetings or back-and-forth emails, allowing the team to stay informed and focused on their tasks.

By automating these aspects of project management, Microsoft 365 Copilot empowers you to focus on strategy and decision-making, rather than getting bogged down by administrative tasks. The result is a more organized, efficient project management process that allows you to deliver results on time and within budget.

3.2.2. AI TOOLS FOR DOCUMENT COLLABORATION AND SHARING

In any organization, document collaboration and sharing are key to maintaining smooth operations. Whether it's working on project reports, proposals, or strategic plans, ensuring that multiple people can contribute to a document in a seamless and organized way is critical. Microsoft 365 Copilot takes document collaboration to the next level by integrating AI-powered tools that streamline the process, reduce errors, and keep everyone on the same page.

Real-Time Document Collaboration

One of the most frustrating aspects of document collaboration is managing multiple versions and ensuring that everyone is working with the most up-to-date information. With Copilot, real-time collaboration becomes easier and more efficient. Whether your team is editing a report in Word, creating a presentation in PowerPoint, or updating a spreadsheet in Excel, Copilot ensures that everyone's changes are tracked and merged into a single, cohesive document.

Imagine you're working with your team on a project proposal that needs input from various departments. Instead of waiting for each person to submit their edits and manually integrating them into the document, you can prompt Copilot with, "Track all changes made to the proposal and summarize key edits." Copilot will not only track each team member's contributions but also provide you with a summary of the significant updates, ensuring that nothing is missed.

This real-time collaboration feature is particularly useful in fast-paced environments where decisions need to be made quickly. Everyone can work simultaneously on the same document, confident that their changes will be reflected in real-time, without the confusion that comes from version control issues.

Automating Document Sharing

When collaborating on important documents, sharing files with the right people at the right time is crucial. Copilot simplifies document sharing by automating this process and ensuring that the right stakeholders have access to the latest version of the file.

For instance, if you're finishing a report and need to send it out for review, you can prompt Copilot with, "Share the latest version of the report with the marketing and finance teams." Copilot will locate the most recent version of the document and share it with the appropriate people, removing the need for you to manually send emails or check who has access.

This feature also helps with permission management. If a document contains sensitive information, you can specify access levels, and Copilot will ensure that only the designated individuals have the appropriate permissions. A prompt like, "Share the financial report with senior leadership only, and set view-only permissions," will handle the task, protecting sensitive data while still allowing collaboration.

Coordinating Feedback and Revisions

One of the most challenging parts of document collaboration is managing feedback from multiple team members. Gathering feedback, addressing comments, and ensuring that revisions are integrated can quickly become overwhelming. Copilot helps by organizing and streamlining the feedback process, so you can focus on refining the content instead of managing edits.

Let's say you've shared a project plan with your team, and now you're receiving comments and suggested changes from different departments. Instead of manually sifting through each comment and trying to keep track of who suggested what, you can ask Copilot to "Summarize feedback on the project plan and group similar suggestions." This way, you'll receive an organized summary of the feedback, with similar comments grouped together, making it easier to address common concerns in a single revision.

Furthermore, Copilot can assist in implementing changes directly. For example, if you've received approval from stakeholders to make certain revisions, you can prompt, "Incorporate the approved changes from the marketing team into the document," and Copilot will apply the changes, ensuring that everyone's input is reflected in the final version.

Version Control and Document History

Maintaining a clear history of document changes is essential for collaboration, especially in large teams or long-term projects. Copilot helps with version control by keeping track of all changes made to a document and allowing you to revert to previous versions if necessary. A simple prompt like, "Show the document history for the last week," will give you an overview of all edits made, who made them, and when they occurred.

This is particularly useful when there are conflicting edits or when a decision is made to return to a previous version of a document. If you need to restore an earlier version, you can prompt, "Revert to the version from three days ago," and Copilot will retrieve the document as it was on that date, ensuring that no critical information is lost.

Copilot also helps prevent duplication of effort by notifying team members when a document is being edited in real-time. This ensures that no one overwrites someone else's work and that all changes are captured without confusion.

Enhancing Security and Compliance

For organizations dealing with sensitive information or operating in industries with strict compliance requirements, ensuring the security of shared documents is critical. Copilot enhances security by allowing you to automate permissions and track document access. If a document contains confidential data, you can prompt Copilot to, "Set access restrictions and track who opens the document," ensuring that only authorized personnel can view or edit the file.

In addition, Copilot can generate audit trails that track who accessed or edited a document and when. A prompt like, "Generate an audit report for the project proposal," will produce a detailed log of all actions taken on the document, helping you ensure compliance with internal policies or external regulations.

Seamless Integration Across Tools

One of Copilot's greatest strengths is its ability to integrate seamlessly with other Microsoft 365 applications. Whether you're working in Word, Excel, PowerPoint, or even Microsoft Teams, Copilot ensures that documents flow effortlessly between tools and users. If you're working on a spreadsheet in Excel and need to present the data in PowerPoint, you can prompt Copilot with, "Create a PowerPoint presentation from this Excel data," and it will automatically generate the slides, complete with charts and graphs.

This integration means that you can move quickly between different tasks and tools without losing context or momentum. Documents, presentations, and spreadsheets can be shared, edited, and presented in a way that feels cohesive and efficient, boosting overall productivity.

With Microsoft 365 Copilot, document collaboration and sharing are no longer burdensome, time-consuming tasks. By automating key processes like sharing, tracking changes, managing feedback, and ensuring security, Copilot allows teams to focus on what really matters—creating high-quality content and driving projects forward. AI-enhanced collaboration means that everyone can contribute efficiently, and documents stay organized and accessible, no matter how many hands are involved.

Chapter 4

4. Real-World Examples

Throughout this book, we've explored how Microsoft 365 Copilot can transform the way we work, from automating tasks to enhancing collaboration and improving workflow efficiency. But theory is one thing—seeing how these tools work in real-world scenarios brings everything to life. In this chapter, we'll dive into specific examples of how businesses and professionals have successfully integrated Copilot into their daily operations, achieving remarkable results.

Whether you're managing a small business, leading a corporate team, or working as an individual professional, these real-world case studies will show you how AI can streamline your work, save time, and increase productivity. From automating repetitive tasks like data analysis and report generation to improving team collaboration through smart tracking and document sharing, these examples highlight the practical ways Copilot can be applied across different industries.

One story that stands out involves a mid-sized marketing agency that dramatically cut down their project turnaround times by integrating Copilot into their workflow. By using Copilot to automate project timelines, allocate tasks, and generate client-facing reports, they were able to reduce time spent on administrative tasks by 30%, allowing them to focus more on creative strategy and client interaction.

In this chapter, you'll discover similar stories of how Copilot is not just a helpful tool but a game-changer for organizations looking to enhance productivity, efficiency, and collaboration. Each case study illustrates a different use of Copilot, giving you concrete ideas on how you can apply these strategies in your own work environment.

4.1. CASE STUDY 1: AI IN CORPORATE ENVIRONMENTS

4.1.1. AUTOMATING REPETITIVE TASKS FOR HR TEAMS

Let's delve into a detailed case study of how Microsoft 365 Copilot transforms the daily operations of a Human Resources (HR) department within a large corporation. Think of this as observing a sophisticated, well-coordinated team where each member works in perfect harmony, thanks to the support of cutting-edge tools that amplify their capabilities. By implementing Copilot, the HR department moves beyond mundane, repetitive tasks, freeing up valuable time to focus on strategic initiatives and employee engagement. I will provide detailed examples of how Copilot streamlines specific HR processes, illustrating the potential of AI to create a more efficient, responsive, and employee-centric work environment. The goal is to demonstrate that these tools are not just theoretical ideas, but rather concrete and ready-to-use solutions to increase the productivity of your teams.

One of the most significant ways Copilot can help an HR department is by automating the initial stages of the recruitment process. Instead of spending hours manually reviewing resumes, you can use a prompt like, "Analyze the resumes for the marketing manager position and identify candidates that meet the minimum requirements, highlighting their key qualifications and experience," and Copilot will provide you with a list of candidates, saving you time and resources. If you need to focus on a specific area you can ask Copilot to, "Analyze the resumes for the software engineer position, focusing on candidates that have a strong background in python programming and cloud computing," and the AI will generate a customized list based on your needs. This allows HR professionals to focus on candidates that are a better fit for the company, and makes the initial screening process more effective, eliminating a significant amount of time spent in manual review.

Copilot also assists with the creation of interview questions. Instead of creating questions from scratch, you can use prompts like, "Generate a list of interview questions for the marketing manager position, including behavioral, technical, and situational questions," and Copilot will provide you with a detailed list. You can also ask Copilot to, "Generate a list of interview questions for the software engineer position, focusing on questions that will evaluate their problem-solving skills and experience with different programming languages," and the AI will generate a tailored set of questions. This feature helps ensure that all candidates are evaluated with a consistent standard, streamlining your process and allowing you to create a more efficient and effective interviewing process. This allows HR professionals to focus on the human aspects of the interview rather than spending too much time preparing questions.

Furthermore, Copilot helps with the management of employee records. Instead of manually updating employee files, you can use a prompt like: "Update the employee records with the latest changes, including new addresses, contact numbers, and emergency contacts," and Copilot will automatically make the necessary adjustments to the database. If you need to update a specific group of employees you can ask Copilot to: "Update the employee records of the marketing department, including their new roles and responsibilities, and include them into the new organizational chart," and it will adjust your database accordingly. Copilot will ensure that all your employee records are accurate and up-to-date, making it easier for the HR department to access the information they need. This functionality also reduces the possibility of human error, saving valuable time and resources.

Copilot can also automate the process of creating employee training programs. Instead of spending hours creating training materials, you can use a prompt like, "Create a training program for new managers, including topics such as leadership, team management, and communication skills, and include links to relevant material available in our knowledge base," and Copilot will generate a complete training program. You can ask Copilot to, "Create a training program for new software engineers, focusing on coding best practices, agile methodologies, and quality control techniques," and it will generate content tailored to your request. This feature helps reduce the time spent in the training development process, while ensuring all programs are comprehensive, consistent, and effective. Finally, Copilot assists in generating HR reports. You can use prompts like: "Create a report on employee satisfaction for the last quarter, including key findings from the employee survey and recommendations for improvement," and Copilot will generate a detailed report. You can also ask

Copilot to, "Create a report about employee turnover, and highlight key trends, and reasons for employee departures, including recommendations to improve employee retention," Copilot will generate the report for you. Copilot allows HR teams to spend less time on manual tasks and more on strategic initiatives, leading to a more engaged and productive workforce.

4.1.2. ENHANCING FINANCIAL REPORTING AND ANALYSIS

Let's now examine how Copilot can transform the often complex and time-consuming tasks of financial reporting and analysis within a corporate environment. Think of this as having a financial expert always available to provide accurate analysis and insights, and making your reports more precise, more efficient, and ultimately, more valuable. I will now focus on how financial departments can use AI to streamline their daily operations, automating tasks and improving the quality of their reports, by offering very specific examples, always keeping in mind that this should be something that can be easily implemented, focusing on daily workflows, in order to demonstrate the true power of AI in real-world scenarios.

One of the most significant ways Copilot helps financial teams is by automating the process of generating financial reports. Instead of manually compiling data from various sources, you can use prompts like, "Create a financial report for the last quarter, including a balance sheet, income statement, and cash flow statement," and Copilot will automatically generate a complete report. If you want to focus on a specific area, you can use a prompt like, "Create a financial report for the last fiscal year, focusing on the performance of the marketing department, including the department's revenue, expenses, and ROI," and Copilot will adjust its report accordingly, saving you valuable time and resources. This not only reduces the time it takes to generate reports but also eliminates the possibility of human error, ensuring the accuracy and reliability of the data.

Copilot also assists in analyzing financial data and identifying trends that might not be apparent on a surface level. Imagine you want to understand the financial performance of a new product line, and instead of manually searching through large spreadsheets, you can use prompts like, "Analyze the sales data for the new product line 'X' and identify trends in revenue, expenses, and profit margins," and Copilot will provide a comprehensive analysis. If you want to understand the impact of a certain strategy, you can ask Copilot to, "Analyze the financial impact of the recent marketing campaign, highlighting the changes in customer acquisition costs and sales conversions," and the AI will generate a detailed analysis, highlighting the most relevant details you need. Copilot's analysis helps you identify key patterns and make informed decisions about budgeting, cost control, and investment opportunities.

Furthermore, Copilot helps in creating budgets by using historical data and trends, which helps to create more accurate and realistic budgets. Instead of manually entering information, you can use a prompt like, "Create a budget for the next fiscal year based on the data from the last three years, and including a 10% increase in marketing expenses," and Copilot will generate a draft budget based on the information you provided. You can ask Copilot to,

"Create a budget for the R&D department, including projected revenue, expenses, and cash flow projections," and the system will adapt to your requests. This feature significantly reduces the time spent in the budget creation process, allowing the financial team to focus on the strategic implications.

Finally, Copilot helps with financial forecasting, and you can use prompts like, "Create a sales forecast for the next quarter based on the current trends and seasonality data," and the system will generate a forecast that you can then adjust to your needs. If you need to be more precise you can ask Copilot to, "Create a financial forecast for the next year, based on historical trends and market conditions, including a range for best-case, worst-case, and expected-case scenario," and Copilot will adjust its response based on the level of detail required, providing a comprehensive forecast. By using Copilot, your financial department can work more efficiently, making faster, and better decisions based on accurate data.

4.2. CASE STUDY 2: SMALL BUSINESSES AND AI

4.2.1. AUTOMATING CUSTOMER COMMUNICATION

For small businesses, customer communication is a crucial aspect of daily operations, but it can also be time-consuming and overwhelming. From responding to inquiries and sending follow-up emails to managing feedback and maintaining customer relationships, these tasks require constant attention. This is where Microsoft 365 Copilot becomes a valuable asset. By automating customer communication, Copilot helps small businesses stay responsive and efficient, while freeing up time for other important tasks like growth strategies and business development.

Automating Response to Customer Inquiries

One of the biggest challenges for small businesses is managing customer inquiries, especially when the team is small, and there's no dedicated customer service department. Whether it's answering questions about product availability, resolving complaints, or sending out detailed information about services, responding to customers in a timely manner is essential for maintaining satisfaction.

With Microsoft 365 Copilot, small businesses can automate much of the customer inquiry process. For example, if you frequently receive the same types of questions from customers—such as inquiries about shipping times, return policies, or pricing—you can create automated responses using Copilot. A prompt like, "Generate responses to common customer questions about shipping policies," will allow Copilot to draft replies that can be customized and sent with minimal input from your team.

Imagine a scenario where you're running an e-commerce store and you receive multiple inquiries about order status. Instead of manually responding to each email, you can prompt Copilot to, "Respond to all customer inquiries about order status with the tracking information." Copilot will pull the relevant data from your system and craft personalized responses that provide customers with the information they need. This level of automation ensures that customers get timely responses, even when your team is busy with other tasks.

Managing Follow-Ups and Customer Engagement

Effective customer engagement requires consistent follow-up—whether it's sending thank-you emails after a purchase, following up on inquiries, or checking in with potential leads. However, manually managing follow-ups can quickly become overwhelming, especially when your customer base grows. This is where Copilot's automation capabilities shine.

For instance, after a customer purchases a product, Copilot can automatically send a follow-up email thanking them for their business and asking for feedback. A prompt like, "Send follow-up emails to customers who purchased in the last week and request feedback," will ensure that every customer receives a personalized message, making them feel valued and helping you gather important insights about their experience.

Additionally, Copilot can help you stay on top of leads and potential customers. If you're tracking leads in Excel or another CRM tool, you can prompt Copilot with, "Follow up with all leads who haven't responded in the last two weeks," and it will generate personalized follow-up emails based on your past communications. This ensures that no opportunities slip through the cracks and that your business remains proactive in its customer engagement efforts.

Streamlining Customer Feedback Collection

Collecting customer feedback is a vital part of improving products and services, but the process of gathering and analyzing feedback can be cumbersome, especially for small businesses without the resources for a dedicated team. Copilot helps streamline this process by automating feedback collection and analysis.

Let's say you want to gather feedback after launching a new product. Instead of manually emailing each customer and compiling their responses, you can prompt Copilot with, "Send a feedback survey to all customers who purchased the new product," and it will handle the communication. Copilot can also track responses, sending reminders to customers who haven't yet completed the survey, ensuring a higher response rate.

Once feedback is collected, Copilot can assist with the analysis as well. A prompt like, "Summarize customer feedback from the latest survey and highlight common suggestions," will provide you with an organized report of the most frequently mentioned points. This helps you quickly identify areas for improvement, whether it's product design, customer service, or delivery times.

Creating Personalized Customer Communications

One of the benefits of Copilot's AI-powered automation is its ability to tailor communications to individual customers. Personalization is key to building strong customer relationships, and with Copilot, you can easily customize emails, newsletters, and updates based on customer behavior and preferences.

For example, if a customer has recently made several purchases or interacted with your business frequently, you can prompt Copilot to, "Send a personalized email to high-value customers offering a discount on their next purchase." Copilot will use the customer's purchase history and engagement data to craft a message that feels personalized, helping you strengthen the relationship and encourage repeat business.

Similarly, if a customer has expressed dissatisfaction or provided negative feedback, Copilot can help you respond in a way that acknowledges their concerns and offers solutions. A prompt like, "Draft a response to this customer's complaint and offer a 10% discount as an apology," ensures that you're addressing the issue promptly and maintaining a positive relationship with your customer base.

Freeing Up Time for Business Growth

By automating routine customer communication tasks, Copilot allows small business owners and employees to focus on what really matters—growing the business. Instead of spending hours each day managing emails, follow-ups, and feedback, your team can invest time in more strategic activities like marketing, product development, and building partnerships.

One small business, a local bakery with a growing online presence, found that by automating their customer communication with Copilot, they were able to reduce the time spent on email management by 50%. This allowed the owner to focus on expanding their product line and building relationships with local suppliers, ultimately leading to increased sales and a more robust customer base.

For small businesses, Microsoft 365 Copilot provides a powerful solution to the challenges of managing customer communication. By automating tasks like responding to inquiries, sending follow-ups, collecting feedback, and personalizing messages, Copilot ensures that customers feel valued and supported, while freeing up valuable time for business owners to focus on growth and development.

4.2.2. STREAMLINING DATA ENTRY AND INVOICING

Data entry and invoicing are essential tasks for any small business, but they can also be some of the most tedious and time-consuming. For many small business owners, managing spreadsheets, inputting customer information, and generating invoices are tasks that take valuable time away from higher-level strategic efforts. This is where Microsoft 365 Copilot comes in, providing powerful automation tools to streamline these processes, reduce errors, and free up time for more critical business operations.

Automating Data Entry

For small businesses, data entry often involves manually inputting customer information, tracking sales, updating inventory, and recording expenses. This process can be not only monotonous but also prone to human error, which can lead to costly mistakes, particularly when dealing with financial records or customer data.

Copilot helps eliminate these manual processes by automating data entry tasks. Imagine running a small retail business where you receive online orders daily. Instead of manually entering each order into your sales tracking system, you can prompt Copilot with, "Automatically input the latest customer orders into the sales tracking sheet." Copilot will extract the relevant data from the order system, update your records, and organize the information in the correct fields—all without you needing to lift a finger.

This automation ensures that your records are always up-to-date and accurate, which is critical for managing your business effectively. Additionally, by reducing the manual workload, you minimize the risk of errors that could lead to issues with inventory management, customer service, or financial reporting.

Efficient Invoicing with Copilot

Generating invoices is another area where Copilot can make a significant difference for small businesses. Whether you're a freelancer billing clients for services or a small retail business processing invoices for bulk orders, the process of creating, sending, and tracking invoices can take a considerable amount of time.

With Copilot, invoicing becomes a seamless and automated task. Let's say you're a freelance graphic designer who bills clients for hourly work. Instead of manually creating an invoice at the end of each project, you can prompt Copilot with, "Generate an invoice for Client X based on the hours logged in the time-tracking sheet." Copilot will pull the hours from your records, calculate the total amount owed, and generate a professional invoice in seconds.

Copilot also helps with automating recurring invoices. If you have clients or customers on a subscription plan, you can set up Copilot to handle the invoicing process on a regular basis. A prompt like, "Send monthly invoices to all subscription clients based on their billing information," will ensure that invoices are sent out on time every month, without you having to manually intervene. This not only saves time but also ensures that you're getting paid promptly and consistently.

Tracking Payments and Follow-Ups

Once invoices are sent, tracking payments and sending reminders to clients who are late on their payments can be a tedious and uncomfortable task. Copilot helps automate this process, ensuring that you stay on top of payments without having to spend hours manually checking records or following up with customers.

For example, you can prompt Copilot with, "Track unpaid invoices and send reminders to clients who are past due." Copilot will review your invoicing system, identify any overdue payments, and automatically send polite reminders to the relevant clients. This allows you to maintain a professional and timely payment collection process without the awkwardness of manually chasing down payments.

In addition, Copilot can generate reports that help you track your cash flow and payment status. A prompt like, "Generate a report of all outstanding invoices and categorize them by payment status," will give you a clear view of your financial situation, helping you make informed decisions about your business.

Simplifying Inventory Management

For small businesses that manage physical inventory, keeping track of stock levels and ensuring that inventory data is accurate is critical to running a smooth operation. Copilot helps automate inventory tracking, ensuring that your records are always up to date.

Imagine you own a small boutique that sells handmade jewelry. Keeping track of how many pieces of each item you have in stock can be a challenge, especially when inventory changes frequently. Instead of manually updating your inventory spreadsheet every time a sale is made or new stock arrives, you can prompt Copilot with, "Update inventory levels based on recent sales data and incoming shipments." Copilot will automatically adjust your inventory records, ensuring that you have an accurate count of what's available.

This automation is particularly helpful for businesses that sell across multiple channels, such as in-store and online. Copilot can integrate with your point-of-sale systems and e-commerce platforms, ensuring that inventory levels are updated in real time across all platforms. This prevents the common issue of overselling products that are out of stock or understocking items that are in high demand.

Freeing Up Time for Business Growth

By automating data entry, invoicing, payment tracking, and inventory management, Microsoft 365 Copilot allows small business owners to reclaim valuable hours each week. This saved time can then be reinvested into growing the business—whether that means focusing on marketing efforts, improving customer service, or developing new products and services.

One small business, a local coffee roastery, reported that after implementing Copilot to automate their invoicing and inventory management processes, they were able to reduce time spent on administrative tasks by 30%. This freed up the owner to focus on expanding their wholesale business, building new relationships with local cafes and restaurants, which led to a 20% increase in revenue over the next quarter.

For small businesses, automating data entry and invoicing with Microsoft 365 Copilot means more than just reducing the workload. It means improving accuracy, ensuring timely payments, and freeing up time to focus on growth. By handling these essential yet repetitive tasks, Copilot allows business owners to spend more time doing what they love and less time on administrative burdens.

Chapter 5

5. Future Trends in AI Productivity Tools

As we've explored throughout this book, AI-driven tools like Microsoft 365 Copilot are already transforming the way we work, automate tasks, and collaborate. But what we've seen so far is only the beginning. The future of AI in productivity tools is poised to be even more revolutionary, with advancements that will reshape industries, redefine workflows, and empower professionals to achieve more than ever before.

In this final chapter, we'll take a closer look at some of the emerging trends in AI productivity tools. From predictive AI that anticipates your needs before you even articulate them, to more advanced machine learning models that can automate entire workflows with minimal input, the future is full of exciting possibilities. These tools won't just help us work faster—they'll help us work smarter by providing deeper insights, automating complex tasks, and even assisting in decision-making processes.

As AI becomes more integrated into the fabric of everyday business, professionals will need to adapt to new ways of working. It won't be enough to simply know how to use AI tools—you'll need to understand how to collaborate with AI, leveraging its capabilities to complement your own expertise. The companies and individuals who are quickest to embrace these trends will have a significant advantage in the marketplace.

In this chapter, we'll explore the key trends shaping the future of AI productivity tools and how they will impact various industries. From predictive analytics to AI-powered decision-making and even AI-driven personal assistants, the next wave of AI will revolutionize how we think about productivity. Let's dive into the future and see what's next for AI and the workplace.

5.1. Emerging AI Technologies

5.1.1. Predictive AI and Personal Assistants

As AI technology continues to advance, one of the most exciting developments is the rise of predictive AI and its integration into personal assistants. Predictive AI takes automation to the next level by anticipating your needs and offering solutions before you even ask. This shift from reactive to proactive AI will reshape how we interact with technology, particularly in workplace productivity tools.

What is Predictive AI?

Predictive AI uses machine learning models that analyze historical data and user behavior to predict future outcomes and actions. In the context of productivity tools, this means AI will not just respond to your commands but will start to predict what you need based on patterns it detects in your work habits. Think of it as having an assistant that not only responds when you give it a task but also proactively offers suggestions and solutions, making your workflow more efficient without you having to ask.

For example, if you consistently run sales reports every Friday afternoon, a predictive AI could learn this pattern and start generating the report automatically, delivering it to your inbox or dashboard without you having to prompt it. If you're preparing for a meeting, it might preemptively gather related documents, pull in key data points, and even draft talking points based on past conversations. This shift from reactive to proactive assistance saves time, reduces friction, and allows professionals to focus on higher-level tasks.

Predictive AI in Microsoft 365

In Microsoft 365, we're already beginning to see predictive AI in action. Tools like Copilot are increasingly able to anticipate user needs based on patterns of behavior, helping automate repetitive tasks and even making suggestions based on your past interactions with the software.

For example, if you regularly review a financial dashboard in Excel every Monday morning, Copilot might start generating the updated dashboard before you log in, presenting it to you with the latest data and key insights, all without requiring a prompt. Similarly, if you're writing emails that frequently include certain attachments, Copilot could automatically suggest including those documents when you draft new messages to related contacts.

Another example of predictive AI is in scheduling and meeting preparation. If Copilot notices that you frequently schedule meetings with a certain team at the same time each week, it might start preemptively suggesting meeting slots, preparing agendas, and even drafting follow-up emails—all based on your usual workflow. This saves you time and ensures that you stay ahead of your tasks without having to micromanage every detail.

AI-Powered Personal Assistants

While we've seen the beginnings of AI-powered personal assistants in tools like Cortana, Alexa, and Google Assistant, the next generation of AI personal assistants will be much more sophisticated. These assistants won't just perform basic tasks like setting reminders or playing music—they'll become deeply integrated into your professional life, helping you manage everything from your calendar to your work projects.

Personal assistants powered by predictive AI will offer more personalized, context-aware suggestions. For example, imagine an AI assistant that not only schedules your meetings but also knows which documents you'll need for the meeting, who the key participants are, and what follow-up actions are likely to be required. A prompt like, "Prepare for tomorrow's meeting," would result in the assistant gathering all relevant materials, sending reminders to attendees, and even creating a draft agenda based on the meeting's topic and past conversations with the team.

As these AI-powered assistants evolve, they will also become more adept at understanding complex tasks and helping with decision-making. Imagine an assistant that could analyze multiple data sets, run simulations, and present you with recommended courses of action based on potential outcomes. For a business leader, this would mean having an AI assistant that not only schedules and organizes but also contributes to strategic decision-making by providing data-driven insights in real time.

The Benefits of Predictive AI and Personal Assistants

The rise of predictive AI and advanced personal assistants will significantly enhance productivity in the workplace. Here are some key benefits:

1. **Time Savings**: Predictive AI reduces the need for manual tasks and routine prompts, allowing you to focus on more important work. By automating the collection of data, generating reports, and anticipating your needs, AI will handle the administrative burden, freeing up your time for strategic and creative tasks.
2. **Reduced Cognitive Load**: With AI handling repetitive tasks and anticipating next steps, professionals will experience less mental fatigue. Rather than spending time thinking about what needs to happen next, you'll be able to trust that your AI assistant is already working in the background to keep you organized and prepared.
3. **Improved Decision-Making**: Predictive AI can analyze large amounts of data quickly and present key insights, helping you make more informed decisions. Instead of digging through spreadsheets or waiting for reports, you'll have real-time access to the information you need to drive your business forward.
4. **Enhanced Personalization**: Because predictive AI learns from your habits, its recommendations become more personalized over time. The more you use these tools, the better they'll understand

your preferences, routines, and priorities, making your interactions with AI more seamless and relevant.

5. **Seamless Integration Across Tools**: As AI-powered personal assistants become more integrated with productivity tools like Microsoft 365, you'll experience a more unified workflow. Whether you're drafting emails, managing projects, or analyzing data, your AI assistant will help ensure that everything is connected, so you don't have to switch between apps or manually track tasks.

The Future of AI in the Workplace

As predictive AI and personal assistants continue to evolve, their role in the workplace will expand. We can expect these tools to take on even more responsibilities, from managing entire projects to making recommendations based on predictive models that account for market trends, financial forecasts, and more. The future of work will be one where professionals and AI work side by side, complementing each other's strengths to achieve greater efficiency and success.

In the near future, AI won't just be a tool you use—it will be a partner in your daily operations, constantly working in the background to anticipate your needs, provide insights, and help you make smarter decisions. For businesses that embrace these emerging technologies, the potential for innovation and growth is limitless.

5.1.2. AI-Driven Decision-Making Tools

As artificial intelligence continues to evolve, one of its most powerful applications in the workplace is assisting with decision-making. AI-driven decision-making tools analyze vast amounts of data in real time, providing insights that help professionals make faster, more informed decisions. These tools can do everything from offering recommendations based on historical data to running complex simulations that forecast the potential outcomes of different decisions. As AI becomes more sophisticated, its role in decision-making will only grow, helping businesses of all sizes become more efficient and data-driven.

What Are AI-Driven Decision-Making Tools?

At their core, AI-driven decision-making tools leverage machine learning algorithms and predictive models to help professionals evaluate different options and choose the best course of action. These tools analyze historical data, current trends, and even external factors like market conditions or customer behavior to provide insights and forecasts. Rather than relying solely on intuition or past experiences, decision-makers can use AI-generated insights to guide their strategy and optimize outcomes.

For example, in a business setting, an AI tool could analyze a company's sales data over the past five years, cross-reference it with current market trends, and recommend the best product to launch next based on predicted demand. The AI would not only provide a recommendation but also back it up with data-driven insights, such as potential revenue projections, customer interest patterns, and competition analysis.

How AI is Enhancing Decision-Making in Microsoft 365

Microsoft 365 Copilot is already making strides in integrating AI-driven decision-making tools into the workplace. By analyzing data across various applications like Excel, Power BI, and Outlook, Copilot can provide professionals with actionable insights that help improve decision-making across a wide range of business functions.

Take budgeting as an example. If you're preparing a budget forecast for the next quarter, you can prompt Copilot with, "Generate a forecast based on the last three years of financial data and current market trends." Copilot will pull data from Excel, analyze it, and provide a detailed budget forecast, highlighting potential risks or opportunities. This kind of AI-driven analysis ensures that your financial decisions are based on hard data rather than assumptions or guesswork.

In addition to forecasting, Copilot can also help with optimizing decisions in real-time. For instance, if you're leading a sales team and want to know which products to focus on during an upcoming promotional campaign, you can ask Copilot, "Which products have the highest potential for increased sales during the holiday season?" Copilot will analyze historical sales data, customer preferences, and market conditions to recommend the products most likely to perform well, enabling you to make more informed decisions.

AI-Powered Scenario Planning and Simulations

One of the most exciting applications of AI-driven decision-making tools is their ability to run scenario planning and simulations. These tools can simulate different strategies or decisions, allowing professionals to see the potential outcomes before they commit to a course of action. This is particularly useful in complex situations where multiple factors are at play, and the consequences of a decision are not immediately obvious.

For example, let's say you're planning a major expansion for your business, and you want to evaluate the financial impact of different strategies—opening a new location, launching a new product line, or entering a new market. With AI-powered scenario planning, you can simulate each of these options. A prompt like, "Simulate the financial outcomes of launching a new product line vs. opening a new location," will have Copilot run the numbers, analyze historical data, and provide projections for each option.

This simulation allows decision-makers to weigh the potential risks and rewards of each strategy before committing resources, helping businesses make smarter, more calculated decisions. It's not just about looking at past data—these tools help you anticipate the future and prepare for different possibilities, making them invaluable for long-term planning.

Automating Routine Decision-Making

In addition to helping with high-level strategic decisions, AI-driven tools are also useful for automating routine decision-making tasks. For example, in supply chain management, AI can help determine optimal inventory levels by analyzing sales patterns, seasonal trends, and supplier data. A prompt like, "Analyze sales trends and suggest optimal inventory levels for the next quarter," allows Copilot to automate the process of setting inventory targets, ensuring that stock levels are neither too high nor too low.

By automating routine decisions like these, AI frees up time for professionals to focus on more complex, high-impact decisions. It also ensures that everyday decisions are made based on data, reducing the risk of human error or bias. This kind of automation is particularly valuable in fast-paced industries where even small delays or miscalculations can have significant financial consequences.

Reducing Bias and Improving Objectivity

One of the major advantages of AI-driven decision-making tools is their ability to reduce bias in the decision-making process. Human decision-making is often influenced by personal biases, whether we realize it or not. These biases can stem from past experiences, preferences, or even subconscious factors, and they can lead to suboptimal decisions.

AI tools, on the other hand, base their recommendations solely on data. By analyzing large datasets and providing insights without the influence of human emotions or biases, AI-driven decision-making tools help ensure that decisions are more objective and based on facts. This can lead to better outcomes, especially in areas like hiring, where unconscious biases can have a significant impact.

For instance, if you're hiring for a new role and want to ensure that your decision is based on objective criteria, you can use AI to analyze candidate data. A prompt like, "Analyze these candidates' qualifications and recommend the best fit for the role," will have Copilot evaluate each candidate's skills, experience, and performance metrics, helping you make a more data-driven hiring decision.

The Future of AI in Decision-Making

As AI continues to evolve, its role in decision-making will become even more sophisticated. We can expect future AI tools to handle increasingly complex decisions, integrating even more data sources and offering deeper insights. From guiding businesses through major strategic shifts to assisting in daily operational decisions, AI-driven decision-making tools will become an indispensable part of the modern workplace.

The future will also likely see AI tools that are capable of not just providing recommendations, but also executing decisions automatically based on predefined parameters. For instance, an AI tool might automatically adjust your marketing spend based on real-time performance data or place inventory orders when stock levels dip below a certain threshold.

In short, AI-driven decision-making tools represent a major leap forward in how businesses operate, allowing for faster, smarter, and more objective decisions that drive growth and efficiency.

5.2. Preparing for the AI-Enhanced Future

5.2.1. Adapting Workflows for New AI Technologies

As AI technologies continue to advance and integrate more deeply into the workplace, businesses and professionals must adapt their workflows to fully harness the potential of these new tools. While AI can offer unprecedented levels of automation, efficiency, and insight, its benefits will only be realized if workflows are reimagined to complement these technologies. In this section, we'll explore how organizations can adapt their existing processes to thrive in an AI-enhanced future.

Rethinking Task Allocation

One of the first steps in adapting workflows for AI is to rethink task allocation. Traditionally, employees have spent significant amounts of time on repetitive, administrative tasks—such as data entry, scheduling, and reporting—that can now be automated with AI. By using AI-powered tools like Microsoft 365 Copilot, businesses can offload these tasks, freeing up employees to focus on more strategic, creative, and high-value activities.

For example, instead of manually generating weekly sales reports, a sales team can prompt Copilot with, "Generate the weekly sales report," allowing them to dedicate more time to customer engagement or strategy sessions. Similarly, routine administrative tasks, such as scheduling meetings, responding to common customer inquiries, or managing inventory, can all be handled by AI, reducing the workload on staff.

Adapting workflows to incorporate AI means thinking critically about what tasks can be automated and redesigning job roles to focus on decision-making, problem-solving, and relationship-building. As more tasks are automated, employees will need to develop new skill sets that emphasize creativity, leadership, and analytical thinking.

Enhancing Collaboration with AI

Collaboration is a core component of any successful organization, and AI tools are making collaboration more seamless than ever. As businesses adapt to an AI-driven future, workflows should be designed to leverage AI's ability to enhance communication and teamwork. Microsoft 365 Copilot, for instance, enables real-time collaboration on documents, automatic summarization of meetings, and tracking of tasks across teams.

Imagine working on a collaborative project with team members in different time zones. Instead of waiting for updates or searching through long email threads, Copilot can be prompted to "Summarize the latest changes to the project document and highlight key points," ensuring that everyone is on the same page and aware of the project's progress. This kind of automation eliminates communication delays and helps keep teams aligned, no matter where they are.

Workflows in the future will need to be designed with AI-powered collaboration in mind. Tools like Copilot can streamline how documents are edited, meetings are organized, and tasks are tracked, allowing teams to work more efficiently and focus on the strategic aspects of their projects.

Integrating AI into Decision-Making Processes

Another area where workflows will need to adapt is in decision-making processes. AI is increasingly being used to provide real-time data, predictive analytics, and insights that help professionals make informed decisions quickly. Incorporating AI into decision-making workflows will require organizations to shift from relying on historical data and manual analysis to using AI-generated insights for more agile and informed choices.

For instance, in a marketing department, instead of manually analyzing campaign data at the end of each quarter, AI tools can continuously monitor performance metrics and suggest adjustments on the fly. A marketing manager might prompt Copilot with, "Analyze the current campaign and suggest optimizations," and receive real-time recommendations based on customer behavior, engagement trends, and sales data. This allows businesses to make faster, data-driven decisions that improve outcomes.

Workflows that incorporate AI for decision-making will need to be flexible, allowing teams to quickly adjust strategies based on the insights provided by AI. This adaptability will be critical as businesses operate in increasingly competitive and fast-moving markets.

Training and Upskilling Employees

As AI tools take on more routine tasks, the role of the human workforce will evolve. Employees will need to focus on the tasks that AI cannot yet perform—such as strategic thinking, complex problem-solving, and emotional intelligence. To prepare for this shift, organizations must invest in training and upskilling their employees.

Training programs should focus on teaching employees how to effectively use AI tools, understand the insights they provide, and integrate them into daily workflows. For example, finance teams can be trained to interpret AI-generated forecasts and use them to develop more robust financial strategies. Marketing teams can learn how to analyze AI-driven customer insights to craft more personalized and effective campaigns.

In addition to technical skills, soft skills like creativity, leadership, and collaboration will become even more important in an AI-enhanced workplace. Employees will need to be able to think critically about the data provided by AI, make decisions based on that data, and work effectively in teams where AI tools play an active role.

Building a Culture of Innovation

To fully adapt to AI technologies, businesses must foster a culture of innovation. AI is rapidly changing the landscape of work, and organizations that encourage experimentation, creativity, and adaptability will be best positioned to take advantage of these changes. Leaders should encourage teams to explore new ways of integrating AI into their workflows and reward innovation.

For example, a company might create cross-functional teams tasked with identifying areas where AI can streamline processes or uncover new business opportunities. These teams can use AI tools to experiment with different approaches, run simulations, and test strategies in a controlled environment. By fostering a culture that embraces AI and encourages continuous learning, businesses can stay ahead of the curve and remain competitive in a rapidly changing landscape.

The Importance of Ethical AI Use

As AI becomes more integrated into workflows, it's crucial that businesses approach its use ethically and responsibly. AI tools have the potential to impact areas such as hiring, decision-making, and customer service, so it's important to ensure that these tools are used in a way that is fair, unbiased, and transparent.

For example, if an AI tool is being used to screen job candidates, businesses should regularly audit the tool to ensure that it is not introducing bias into the hiring process. Organizations should also be transparent with employees and customers about how AI is being used, ensuring that trust is maintained as these technologies become more prevalent.

As AI technologies continue to reshape the workplace, adapting workflows to incorporate these tools will be essential for maintaining efficiency and staying competitive. By rethinking task allocation, enhancing collaboration, integrating AI into decision-making, and upskilling employees, businesses can position themselves for success in the AI-enhanced future.

5.2.2. TRAINING TEAMS TO WORK WITH AI

TeAs AI becomes a key driver of productivity and efficiency in the workplace, one of the most critical factors in realizing its full potential will be the ability of employees to work effectively with these new tools. While AI can automate many tasks, its true value comes from being integrated into workflows and decision-making processes, guided by humans who understand how to leverage its capabilities. Training teams to work with AI will be essential for organizations aiming to stay competitive and innovative in the AI-enhanced future.

Building AI Literacy

The first step in preparing teams to work with AI is to build foundational AI literacy. This doesn't mean that every employee needs to become a data scientist, but they should have a solid understanding of what AI is, how it works, and how it can be applied in their roles. AI literacy empowers employees to see AI not as a threat, but as a powerful tool that can help them do their jobs more efficiently and creatively.

Training programs should focus on helping employees understand key AI concepts, such as machine learning, natural language processing, and predictive analytics. These concepts are the backbone of AI tools like Microsoft 365 Copilot, and understanding them allows employees to better interact with these systems. A basic grasp of how AI makes decisions or generates insights will help employees trust AI outputs and use them to inform their work.

Additionally, AI literacy should include education about the ethical implications of AI. Employees need to be aware of the potential for bias in AI algorithms and understand the importance of ensuring that AI tools are used fairly and responsibly within the organization.

Hands-On Training with AI Tools

Once employees understand the fundamentals of AI, the next step is to provide hands-on training with the specific AI tools they will be using in their daily workflows. For example, if your organization has implemented Microsoft 365 Copilot, training should focus on how to use Copilot effectively in tools like Word, Excel, and PowerPoint. Employees should learn how to craft prompts, interpret AI-generated insights, and integrate AI suggestions into their work processes.

Hands-on training is essential for helping employees gain confidence in working with AI. The more comfortable they are using these tools, the more likely they are to embrace AI as a core part of their job. For instance, employees could practice using Copilot to automate report generation in Excel, draft emails in Outlook, or prepare presentations in PowerPoint. Real-world practice helps employees see immediate benefits, such as time saved on repetitive tasks and improved accuracy in their work.

It's also important to tailor AI training to different roles within the organization. While general AI training is useful for all employees, different teams may use AI tools in unique ways. For example, marketing teams might need training on how to use AI to analyze customer data and optimize campaigns, while finance teams could focus on using AI to automate budgeting and forecasting processes. By customizing training to the specific needs of each department, organizations can ensure that employees are getting the most relevant and impactful AI training.

Encouraging a Growth Mindset

AI is constantly evolving, and the tools employees use today will continue to improve and expand in their capabilities. To ensure that teams are able to keep up with these changes, organizations must foster a culture of continuous learning and encourage employees to adopt a growth mindset. A growth mindset—embracing the belief that skills and abilities can be developed through effort and learning—will be critical in helping employees adapt to new AI tools and updates as they emerge.

Training programs should include ongoing learning opportunities, such as AI workshops, webinars, and online courses, that allow employees to deepen their knowledge over time. This approach not only keeps employees up to date with the latest AI advancements but also empowers them to explore new ways of integrating AI into their work. By encouraging employees to experiment with AI and discover new applications, organizations can create an environment of innovation and adaptability.

Fostering Collaboration Between Humans and AI

As AI becomes more integrated into daily work, it's essential to emphasize the idea of collaboration between humans and AI. AI tools like Copilot are not meant to replace human workers but to complement their skills and enhance their capabilities. Training programs should teach employees how to work alongside AI, understanding when to rely on AI-generated insights and when to apply human judgment and creativity.

For example, an AI tool might suggest optimizations for a marketing campaign, but it's up to the marketing team to decide whether those suggestions align with the brand's voice and goals. Similarly, while AI can automate data analysis, it's still up to finance teams to interpret the results and make strategic decisions based on their expertise. By fostering collaboration between humans and AI, organizations can maximize the potential of both.

Leadership's Role in AI Adoption

Leadership plays a critical role in the successful adoption of AI within an organization. Leaders must not only champion AI adoption but also actively participate in AI training programs themselves. When employees see leadership embracing AI tools, they are more likely to follow suit and view AI as an important part of the company's future.

Leaders should also encourage open communication about AI adoption, providing a platform for employees to ask questions, share concerns, and offer suggestions about how AI can be better integrated into the workplace. This open dialogue helps ensure that employees feel supported and empowered as they learn to work with AI.

Measuring the Impact of AI Training

To ensure the effectiveness of AI training programs, organizations should implement metrics to measure their impact. This might include tracking improvements in productivity, reductions in time spent on repetitive tasks, or increases in the quality of work output. Surveys and feedback from employees can also provide valuable insights into how AI is being used and where additional training might be needed.

By continuously evaluating the success of AI training initiatives, organizations can refine their programs and ensure that employees are equipped to take full advantage of AI tools in their roles.

Training teams to work effectively with AI is a critical step in preparing for the AI-enhanced future. By building AI literacy, providing hands-on training, fostering a growth mindset, and encouraging collaboration between humans and AI, organizations can ensure that their employees are ready to embrace the opportunities that AI brings and contribute to a more productive and innovative workplace.

CONCLUSION

As we conclude this journey through the world of Microsoft 365 Copilot and AI-driven productivity tools, it's clear that we are on the cusp of a new era in the workplace. AI is no longer a futuristic concept—it's here, integrated into the tools we use every day, transforming how we work, collaborate, and make decisions. From automating repetitive tasks to enhancing collaboration and providing real-time insights, AI is empowering professionals across industries to work smarter, not harder.

The examples and case studies throughout this book have shown how businesses, both large and small, can harness the power of AI to drive efficiency, improve accuracy, and ultimately achieve better results. Whether it's automating customer communication for a small business or streamlining financial reporting in a corporate environment, AI has proven to be a game-changer in countless ways.

However, the most exciting part of this journey is that we've only just scratched the surface. The future of AI is full of promise, with new technologies like predictive AI and advanced decision-making tools set to further revolutionize the workplace. As we move forward, it will be essential for professionals and organizations to adapt to these changes, upskill their teams, and foster a culture that embraces innovation.

In this rapidly evolving landscape, those who are quick to adopt AI tools and integrate them into their workflows will gain a significant competitive advantage. The future belongs to those who can leverage the power of AI to work more efficiently, make data-driven decisions, and innovate in ways that were previously unimaginable.

KEY TAKEAWAYS ON MICROSOFT 365 COPILOT

SUMMARY OF AI PROMPTS AND TASK AUTOMATION

As we reflect on the powerful capabilities of Microsoft 365 Copilot, one of the key takeaways is its transformative impact on task automation through AI-driven prompts. By allowing professionals to offload routine and repetitive tasks, Copilot has fundamentally changed how we approach our work, helping us achieve more in less time. The beauty of Copilot lies in its simplicity—by using clear and concise prompts, users can command the AI to perform tasks that would otherwise require significant time and effort.

AI Prompts: A New Way to Work

At the heart of Microsoft 365 Copilot is its ability to respond to user prompts, which turns everyday requests into powerful actions. Whether it's generating a report, drafting an email, or analyzing data, AI-powered prompts allow users to focus on higher-level tasks while the AI handles the details. The simplicity of using natural language commands means that professionals don't need specialized technical skills to leverage the full power of Copilot.

For example, instead of manually preparing a report, a user can prompt, "Generate a quarterly sales report," and

Copilot will automatically pull in the relevant data, create charts, and format the report according to the user's needs. This not only saves time but also ensures that tasks are completed with consistency and accuracy. Prompts like, "Summarize today's meeting notes," or "Draft an email to follow up with clients," further streamline daily operations, allowing professionals to work more efficiently.

One of the most impactful aspects of Copilot is its ability to integrate across multiple Microsoft 365 applications, from Word to Excel, PowerPoint, Outlook, and Teams. This means that regardless of where you are working, you can use AI prompts to automate tasks and simplify workflows, making Copilot an indispensable tool in the modern workplace.

Task Automation: Reducing the Administrative Burden

The automation of routine tasks is one of the standout features of Microsoft 365 Copilot. For years, professionals have struggled with balancing their workload—spending hours each week on administrative tasks like organizing data, scheduling meetings, or responding to emails. These tasks, though essential, often take time away from more strategic or creative work. Copilot changes that dynamic by automating these administrative burdens, giving professionals more time to focus on what really matters.

One of the primary ways Copilot does this is by automating document creation and editing. For instance, instead of spending hours formatting a lengthy report or checking for grammar errors, a simple prompt like, "Format this report for presentation," or "Check this document for grammar and style consistency," allows Copilot to handle the task.

This ensures that the final product is polished and professional, without requiring the user to spend excessive time on manual revisions.

Another area where Copilot excels is in automating data analysis. Whether you're managing financial data in Excel or tracking project progress in Power BI, Copilot can quickly analyze data sets, generate insights, and create visualizations. A prompt such as, "Analyze the sales data and generate a summary of top-performing regions," allows Copilot to do the heavy lifting, providing you with actionable insights in a fraction of the time it would take manually.

Enhancing Productivity Across Applications

What makes Copilot especially powerful is its ability to enhance productivity across the entire Microsoft 365 suite. In Outlook, for example, Copilot can manage email correspondence by drafting responses, organizing your inbox, and scheduling meetings. In Teams, it can summarize conversations, track follow-up tasks, and send reminders. In PowerPoint, Copilot can create professional-looking presentations based on content from Word or Excel, reducing the time it takes to prepare for meetings or client presentations.

For many professionals, switching between different applications throughout the day can lead to inefficiencies. Copilot's integration across platforms ensures a smoother, more cohesive workflow, allowing users to move seamlessly between tasks. This integration means that prompts can be given at any stage of the workday, making it easier to stay productive and organized.

For instance, a marketing professional could use Copilot to automate campaign tracking by prompting, "Generate a weekly report of campaign performance and send it to the team." With this single prompt, Copilot would analyze the data in Excel, generate a report, and distribute it via email or Teams, all without requiring the user to manage each step individually. This holistic approach to task automation is what sets Copilot apart as a tool for boosting productivity.

Saving Time and Increasing Accuracy

One of the most significant benefits of using Microsoft 365 Copilot for task automation is the time saved. By automating repetitive and time-consuming tasks, professionals can reclaim hours of their day to focus on high-value activities like strategy, problem-solving, and innovation. This shift not only increases productivity but also reduces stress and burnout, as employees are no longer bogged down by tedious, manual work.

Additionally, AI-driven task automation improves accuracy. When handling data, documents, or communications, human error is always a risk—especially when tasks are repetitive or completed under tight deadlines. Copilot reduces these risks by ensuring that tasks are carried out with precision, whether it's organizing a spreadsheet, drafting a client proposal, or preparing an invoice.

For example, a finance team that traditionally spends hours reconciling budgets and generating financial reports can use Copilot to automate these processes. With prompts like, "Reconcile the Q3 budget and generate a summary report," Copilot handles the complex calculations and data organization, delivering a precise, error-free result. This not only saves time but also ensures that financial data is accurate and reliable.

Looking Ahead: The Future of Task Automation

As AI technology continues to evolve, the future of task automation looks even more promising. Predictive AI, which anticipates user needs before prompts are given, will further enhance productivity by automating tasks preemptively based on patterns and behavior. We are moving toward a future where AI will not just respond to our requests but will also foresee what needs to be done and take action accordingly.

With tools like Microsoft 365 Copilot leading the way, businesses and professionals can look forward to a future where task automation becomes even more intelligent, intuitive, and indispensable.

LONG-TERM BENEFITS OF AI INTEGRATION

As businesses and professionals continue to integrate Microsoft 365 Copilot into their workflows, the long-term benefits of AI integration become increasingly apparent. AI isn't just a temporary trend—it's transforming how work gets done, leading to lasting improvements in efficiency, decision-making, and overall productivity. By embedding AI into daily operations, organizations can unlock a range of long-term advantages that not only streamline current processes but also set the stage for future innovation and growth.

Sustained Efficiency and Time Savings

One of the most immediate and noticeable long-term benefits of integrating AI into the workplace is sustained efficiency. AI tools like Microsoft 365 Copilot automate routine and repetitive tasks, significantly reducing the time spent on administrative duties. Over time, this cumulative time-saving effect allows employees to focus more on high-impact, strategic initiatives, ultimately leading to greater productivity and a better use of resources.

For instance, by automating data entry, report generation, or document editing, businesses can eliminate the hours previously dedicated to these tasks each week. Instead, employees can dedicate that time to tasks that require human insight, such as creative problem-solving, project planning, or relationship-building with clients. Over the long term, this shift in focus results in a more engaged and efficient workforce, with less burnout from manual, repetitive tasks.

Additionally, the more AI is integrated into workflows, the more refined and efficient those processes become. As AI learns from user behavior and adapts to the needs of the organization, it can anticipate tasks and complete them more quickly. This ongoing efficiency means that businesses not only save time today but continue to operate more efficiently as AI becomes better at understanding and responding to their unique workflows.

Enhanced Decision-Making Through Data Insights

AI integration also provides long-term benefits in decision-making. Microsoft 365 Copilot and similar tools are not just automating tasks—they are collecting and analyzing vast amounts of data, generating insights that empower professionals to make more informed decisions. Over time, these AI-generated insights become a critical asset for businesses, offering deeper understanding and foresight into operations, customer behavior, financial performance, and market trends.

For example, a sales team using Copilot to track and analyze sales data can benefit from AI's ability to identify trends and patterns that might not be immediately visible through manual analysis. By continuously analyzing this data, Copilot can predict future sales trends, suggest areas for improvement, or highlight potential risks. This capability enables decision-makers to respond proactively rather than reactively, adjusting strategies based on real-time data.

Long-term, this level of AI-driven insight enhances the decision-making process across all departments—from marketing and operations to finance and customer service. The ability to make data-driven decisions quickly and accurately helps businesses remain agile and competitive in an increasingly fast-paced and data-rich environment.

Scalability and Adaptability

Another significant long-term benefit of AI integration is scalability. As businesses grow, their operations become more complex, and managing that complexity can be challenging. AI tools like Microsoft 365 Copilot are inherently scalable, meaning they can adapt to the needs of both small businesses and large enterprises without requiring a significant overhaul of workflows or processes.

For small businesses, this means that AI can help them operate with the same level of efficiency as larger competitors, leveling the playing field. Copilot allows small teams to handle more work without needing to hire additional staff, automating tasks like customer communication, invoicing, and data management. As these businesses grow, they can continue to rely on AI to scale their operations seamlessly.

For larger organizations, AI integration offers a way to manage increasing complexity. As the number of employees, customers, and data points grows, AI can help organize and streamline operations, ensuring that the business runs smoothly. AI tools can adapt to handle larger datasets, more complex workflows, and greater demand, ensuring that scalability doesn't come at the cost of efficiency.

Improved Employee Satisfaction and Engagement

One of the often-overlooked long-term benefits of AI integration is its positive impact on employee satisfaction and engagement. By automating the more mundane, repetitive aspects of work, AI tools like Copilot free employees to focus on tasks that are more fulfilling and engaging. Employees can spend more time on creative problem-solving, strategic initiatives, and customer interactions, leading to a more enriching work experience.

Furthermore, AI tools reduce the risk of burnout by easing the pressure of tight deadlines and large workloads. When employees aren't bogged down by administrative tasks, they can work at a more sustainable pace, improving their overall well-being and job satisfaction. Over time, this leads to higher employee retention rates, a more positive workplace culture, and a stronger, more engaged workforce.

Encouraging Innovation and Continuous Improvement

AI tools like Microsoft 365 Copilot foster a culture of innovation within organizations. By automating routine tasks, AI frees up time for employees to experiment, innovate, and pursue new ideas. This focus on continuous improvement becomes ingrained in the organizational culture as employees are encouraged to explore new ways of integrating AI into their workflows and finding more efficient ways to achieve their goals.

Over the long term, this innovation-driven mindset helps businesses stay ahead of the curve. Organizations that embrace AI integration are more likely to adapt quickly to market changes, adopt new technologies, and identify emerging opportunities. By continuously improving and refining their processes with the help of AI, these businesses remain competitive and innovative in a rapidly evolving business landscape.

Cost Savings and Operational Efficiency

Finally, one of the most tangible long-term benefits of AI integration is the cost savings it can provide. By automating tasks that would otherwise require significant human labor, businesses can reduce operational costs without sacrificing quality. AI-driven automation allows businesses to operate with greater efficiency, reducing the need for additional hires while maintaining or even increasing productivity levels.

In addition to reducing labor costs, AI tools like Copilot can help businesses avoid costly mistakes. By automating data entry, financial reporting, and compliance tasks, AI minimizes the risk of human error, which can lead to costly rework, penalties, or lost opportunities.

Over time, these cost savings compound, allowing businesses to invest in growth, innovation, and employee development.

By embracing Microsoft 365 Copilot and other AI-driven tools, businesses can unlock a wide range of long-term benefits. From sustained efficiency and better decision-making to scalability, employee engagement, and cost savings, AI integration paves the way for a more productive, innovative, and competitive future.

FINAL THOUGHTS ON THE FUTURE OF AI IN PRODUCTIVITY

WHAT'S NEXT FOR MICROSOFT 365 AND AI?

As we look to the future, it's clear that the integration of AI into productivity tools like Microsoft 365 is just the beginning of a much larger transformation in how we work. AI has already demonstrated its ability to streamline workflows, automate tasks, and enhance decision-making, but the next wave of AI advancements will push these capabilities even further, creating new opportunities for businesses and professionals alike.

The Evolution of AI in Microsoft 365

Microsoft has been at the forefront of AI integration in the workplace, and with tools like Microsoft 365 Copilot, they've shown how AI can make everyday tasks more efficient and impactful. But what's next? The future of Microsoft 365 and AI will likely focus on deeper integration, where AI becomes an even more intuitive and indispensable part of the workplace.

One area where we can expect to see significant advancement is in predictive AI. As AI becomes better at understanding user behavior and preferences, tools like Copilot will begin to anticipate your needs, offering suggestions and automating tasks before you even think to ask. This next generation of AI will use data from your past interactions, task history, and patterns of work to proactively assist you, providing even greater efficiency and reducing the need for manual input.

For example, if you regularly run a specific report every Monday morning, future iterations of Copilot might start generating that report automatically, delivering it to your inbox or dashboard without any prompting. Similarly, if you often collaborate with certain team members on projects, Copilot might automatically suggest relevant documents, assign tasks, or schedule meetings based on your ongoing activities. This kind of predictive AI will save even more time and effort, allowing professionals to focus on higher-level thinking and strategy.

AI-Driven Personalization and Customization

Another exciting development on the horizon is greater personalization of AI tools. As AI learns more about how individual users work, it will offer increasingly tailored recommendations and solutions. This means that Microsoft 365 will not just be a one-size-fits-all platform—it will adapt to the unique needs, preferences, and workflows of each user.

For example, imagine a version of Copilot that can adjust its suggestions based on your personal work style. If you prefer concise, high-level summaries, Copilot might automatically generate shorter, to-the-point reports for you, whereas someone else who prefers more detailed analysis might receive longer, more comprehensive summaries. This kind of AI-driven customization will make Microsoft 365 even more effective by ensuring that the AI adapts to you, rather than the other way around.

We can also expect AI to play a more significant role in personalizing user interfaces. As AI becomes more adept at learning how you interact with tools, it might start rearranging your workspace in Microsoft 365 to prioritize the features and functions you use most frequently. Over time, this could lead to a more streamlined, intuitive experience that minimizes distractions and maximizes productivity.

AI-Enhanced Collaboration and Communication

The future of Microsoft 365 and AI will also see enhanced collaboration capabilities. Today, Copilot can already help teams stay aligned by automating meeting summaries, tracking tasks, and facilitating document collaboration. However, the next generation of AI will take team collaboration to a new level by enabling more intelligent, real-time interactions between team members and across departments.

One exciting possibility is the use of AI to facilitate cross-functional collaboration. Imagine Copilot acting as an intermediary between different teams, automatically synthesizing information from various departments and presenting a unified view to leadership. For example, Copilot could gather data from marketing, sales, and product development teams and generate a comprehensive report that highlights how each department's efforts are contributing to company-wide goals. This kind of cross-departmental intelligence would allow businesses to make more informed, cohesive decisions, and streamline communication between different teams.

Additionally, as remote and hybrid work models become more common, AI will play a crucial role in maintaining strong communication channels. Future AI tools might be able to automatically schedule meetings based on team members' availability across time zones, track project progress in real-time, and even predict potential bottlenecks before they happen, ensuring that teams stay connected and on track no matter where they are located.

Ethical AI and Responsible Use

As AI becomes more embedded in the workplace, there will also be an increasing emphasis on the ethical use of AI. Microsoft has already committed to developing AI technologies that are transparent, accountable, and fair, and this focus will only intensify as AI continues to evolve.

The future of AI in Microsoft 365 will likely include more robust mechanisms for ensuring that AI is used responsibly, particularly in areas like hiring, performance evaluations, and customer interactions. For instance, businesses might use AI to screen job candidates, but there will be a need for transparent auditing processes to ensure that the AI is not introducing bias or discrimination into hiring decisions.

Organizations will need to establish clear guidelines for how AI is used and how data is collected, analyzed, and acted upon. Ensuring that AI remains a force for good will be critical as these tools become even more powerful and integral to business operations.

As we conclude our exploration of Microsoft 365 Copilot and the future of AI in productivity, it's important to shift focus from the potential of these tools to the actions we need to take now. AI has arrived, and it's changing the way we work, collaborate, and solve problems. However, the extent to which you benefit from these advancements depends on your willingness to embrace AI tools, integrate them into your workflows, and continuously learn and adapt.

A Personal Message and Acknowledgements

I want to extend a heartfelt thank you to my family for their unwavering support and encouragement, and to my colleagues for their invaluable insights and collaboration throughout this journey.

To you readers, thank you for taking the time to explore the exciting world of AI and Microsoft 365 Copilot with me. I hope this journey has inspired you to embrace AI as a powerful tool in your own work, helping you achieve more with less effort. Writing this book has been a labor of love, driven by my passion for helping professionals unlock their full potential with cutting-edge technology.

If this book has sparked new ideas, made your work a little easier, or simply opened your eyes to the possibilities of AI, I'd love to hear your thoughts. Your feedback means the world to me, and it helps shape future content that can better serve you.

Please feel free to leave a comment or review—your voice is invaluable in this conversation. Thank you again for your time and trust.

Savannah Johnson